Marriage

A Complete Solution

A simplified guidance towards understanding
Marital Laws in Islām

MAKKI MASJID & MADRASA
75 Stafford Road
Handsworth
BIRMINGHAM.
B21 9DU.
Tel: 0121 551 7417

BY

Shaykh Mufti Saiful Islām

JKN Publications

© Copyright by JKN Publications

First Published in November 2011
Second Edition December 2015

ISBN: 978-0-9565504-8-4

British Library Cataloguing in Publication Data
A catalogue record for this book is available from the British Library.

Publisher's Note:

Every care and attention has been put into the production of this book. If however, you find any errors they are our own, for which we seek Allāh's ﷻ forgiveness and reader's pardon.

Published by:

JKN Publications
118 Manningham Lane
Bradford
West Yorkshire
BD8 7JF
United Kingdom

t: +44 (0) 1274 308 456 l w: www.jkn.org.uk l e: info@jkn.org.uk

Author: Shaykh Mufti Saiful Islām

Printed by Mega Printing in Turkey

"In the Name of Allāh, the Most Beneficent,
the Most Merciful"

Contents

Introduction

In the name of Allāh ﷻ the Most Gracious, the Most Merciful. Praise be to Allāh ﷻ the Lord of the worlds and may peace and blessings be upon His final Messenger Muhammad ﷺ, upon his noble family, his Companions and upon those who follow their path until the final hour.

Every human being by nature is created with sexual desires. In order for an individual to maintain equilibrium in his life, he ought to fulfil his desires in the correct manner. Natural desires of a human being is virtually impossible to eradicate no matter how much effort is made. For this purpose, Allāh ﷻ in His infinite mercy has made lawful for man and woman to derive pleasure from one another through conjugal relationship. Nevertheless, marriage in an Islamic perspective is not merely restricted to satisfying oneself, but is also surrounded by many responsibilities.

One of the distinguishing features of Islām compared to other ideologies and religions is that Islām is not merely a religion catering for the spiritual aspect only (which is unfortunately understood by many today). Rather, it is a complete code of conduct, a Deen that encompasses every aspect of a human being's life. It has set guidelines on how to discharge one's duties correctly in accordance with the Islamic Law.

Islām regards marriage as a great act of worship because it is a responsible affair and a means of preventing a person from many forms of sins i.e. fornication, casting of the gaze upon unlawful things etc. Islām has explained in great details the concept of marriage and all what is affiliated to it. Allāh 🕮 sent the Holy Prophet 🕮 to this earth to complete and perfect His religion. It was amongst the miracles of the Holy Prophet 🕮 that he attained completeness and perfection in every sphere of life which contain many lessons and beautiful examples to learn from. Allāh 🕮 states in the Holy Qur'ān in Sūrah Al-Ahzāb:

$$لَقَدْ كَانَ لَكُمْ فِىْ رَسُوْلِ اللهِ اُسْوَةٌ حَسَنَةٌ$$

Verily for you there is in the Messenger of Allāh
an excellent example. (33: 21)

As far as marital affair is concerned the Messenger of Allāh 🕮 too attained perfection. Allāh 🕮 through the illustrious life of His beloved Messenger 🕮 has presented to us a simple but comprehensive way of achieving the status of a peaceful marriage. Marriage brings about maturity within the couple and makes them responsible people. This will inevitably transpire wisdom and maturity within oneself.

Inspite of the fact that marriage is supposed to be a peaceful and a tranquil affair, today it has become a very questionable matter irrespective of one's religion, ethnicity, gender and prosperity. It has now become a disturbing and worrying occasion. Marriage breakdown, domestic violence etc have unfortunately become endemic amongst the Muslim community. Today marriage is viewed by some people as a difficult affair and responsible for destroying the harmony within family relationships.

Furthermore, commemorating a marriage ceremony of the newly wedded couple has become a financial burden. Islām has always encouraged a simple wedding ceremony. Things such as purchasing expensive and glamorous clothes, appeasing others for maintaining un-islamic family traditions, maintaining one's respect in the eyes of others whilst violating the Laws of Allāh 🖈, entertainment such as music and dancing in wedding functions, hiring expensive cars and halls that are beyond one's needs, baseless customs and extravagance have unfortunately prevailed and taken precedence in the lives of many Muslims today over the blessed teachings of Islām. All of this has resulted due to the negligence and ignorance of the Deen.

Having to adopt such customs would inevitably bring about destruction and many predicaments in our social and domestic life. This notion and mentality reflects upon our abandonment of the beautiful religion, Islām.

Another common reason that brings about many problems within our marriage, is not seeking the right qualities within the prospective partner. Rather than prioritising the Deen and character, people often primarily focus on the family background; the caste, the language, beauty and wealth. It is upsetting that people overlook the noble teachings of our beloved Prophet 🖈 for the sake of other ways of life and making them as their prime standard. It is the teachings of the Holy Qur'ān that we ought to view and follow, by making the exemplary character of the Holy Prophet 🖈 a prime standard in our everyday lives. Due to our negligence, we do not make the time to study the practical ways of the Holy Prophet 鷺, especially in his mutual conduct towards his noble wives. If one was to study the cordial relationship of the Holy Prophet 鷺 with his noble wives, one would be astounded with his remarkable teachings. Even certain Non-Muslim personalities after studying his noble life accept the fact that he was the most amazing personality ever to appear in history.

In this day and age society has reached a point where religion is viewed as a private matter and restricted to one's innerself, home and place of worship. Religion has no part in anything related to the secular life. This deplorable mentality has unfortunately infiltrated into the hearts and minds of many of our Muslim brothers and sisters who are now beginning to view Islām in the same way. Islām is a unique religion and is different in comparison to other religions and ideologies. It is a complete and comprehensively preserved Deen since the last fourteen centuries. During the advent of Islām, the Arabs were living in the dark ages and had no code of conduct to follow. Islām then re-emerged and taught mankind how to live and become complete human beings. What others are beginning to discover and realise now, Islām has taught over fourteen hundred years ago. There are many examples such as hygiene, medicine, science, social etiquettes, disposition, laws of marriage and many more. Hence, Islām cannot be viewed as a private affair since it provides the foundation and guidelines to all worldly needs. We should appreciate Islām as our divine religion and strive to inculcate all its teachings into our day to day lives. We must treat Islām as our only standard and the source of solutions to our daily problems, especially in relation to marriage issues. As mentioned earlier, due to us discarding the Islamic Law we have sadly become ignorant of our religion which has led to this social and moral decline. Many people are unaware of the basic rights of the husband and wife, the children, the Islamic method of nurturing children etc.

Taking the above into account, after careful consideration, Shaykh Mufti Saiful Islām (may Allāh ﷻ preserve him and prolong his life) decided to compile this book with the purpose of educating our brothers and sisters the basic laws of marriage life. It includes its importance, the Islamic method of conducting the marriage, rules that pertain to sexual relationships, the rights of both the husband and wife, general advice, divorce issues, the rights of children and much more. Everything that is included in this book has been researched and compiled under the supervision, instruction and guidance of Shaykh Mufti Saiful Islām Sāhib.

This book has been designed to provide the fundamental teachings and guidelines of all what relates to the marital life in a simplified English language. It encapsulates in a nutshell all the marriage laws mentioned in many of the main reference books in order to facilitate their understanding and implementation. I pray to Allāh ﷻ that He accepts this work and makes it beneficial for our brothers and sisters. Āmeen

Mufti Abdul Waheed
Teacher of Fiqh at Jāmiah Khātamun Nabiyyeen
November 2011/Dhul-Hijjah 1432

Chapter One – The Importance and Virtues of Marriage

■ Marriage is a great blessing from Allāh ﷻ wherein a man and a woman form a union in the form of wedlock. They become permissible to derive pleasure from one another and relatively, become life partners and share each other's happiness, pleasure, joy and sorrow. There are many Deeni (religious) and worldly benefits in marriage if it is done in the correct manner and in conformity with the Islamic Law.

■ Marriage transpires a unique affection and bond between the husband and wife. Allāh ﷻ states in the Holy Qur'ān;

$$ وَمِنْ اٰیٰتِهٖ اَنْ خَلَقَ لَکُمْ مِّنْ اَنْفُسِکُمْ اَزْوَاجًا لِّتَسْکُنُوْا اِلَیْهَا وَجَعَلَ بَیْنَکُمْ مَّوَدَّةً وَّرَحْمَةً $$

Translation: And it is amongst His signs that He has created for you from amongst yourselves wives so that you may find tranquillity in them and He has established love and mercy between you. (30: 21)

Sayyidunā Abdullāh Ibn Abbās ؓ relates that the Holy Prophet ﷺ said, "You shall not find an example of any two mutual lovers that is equal to marriage." (Mishkāt)

■ Below are some Ahādeeth relating to the importance and virtues of marriage.

1. Sayyidunā Anas Ibn Mālik ؓ relates that once, three Com-

12

panions came to the house of (one of) the wives of the Holy Prophet ﷺ inquiring about the worship of the Holy Prophet ﷺ. When they were informed it seemed insufficient to them. They said, "Where are we (in comparison) to the Holy Prophet ﷺ as Allāh ﷻ has forgiven all his past and future sins." So one of them asserted, "As for me I am going to perform Salāh throughout the night permanently (without retiring to bed)." The second Companion asserted, "I am going to fast throughout the year and will not miss a single fast." The third Companion said, "I will disassociate myself from women and will never marry." The Holy Prophet ﷺ (after being informed) approached them and asked, "Are you the ones who said such and such things? By Allāh ﷻ I am the most fearful of Allāh ﷻ and the most pious towards Him, however I fast and break my fast, I perform Salāh (at night) and sleep and I also marry women, so whomsoever diverts from my Sunnah is not from amongst me." (Bukhāri)

2. Marriage is a means of repelling many illicit acts for instance fornication, casting unlawful glances and adultery. The Holy Prophet ﷺ said, "O group of youth! Whosoever amongst you has (adequate) means of marrying then he ought to do so because it lowers the gaze and protects the chastity. But whosoever does not have the ability should fast for indeed it would serve as a protection for him."

(Bukhāri)

3. The Holy Prophet ﷺ is also reported to have said, "The entire world is a place of commodity and the best commodity (that one can have) is a pious wife." (Muslim)

4. Marriage was not merely the Sunnah of the Holy Prophet
   ﷺ but also the Sunnah of all the Prophets ﷺ. It is related
   in Tirmizi by Sayyidunā Abū Ayyūb Al-Ansāri ؓ that the
   Holy Prophet ﷺ said, "Four matters are from amongst the
   Sunnats of all the Prophets ﷺ:

   a) To have Hayā (modesty and bashfulness).
   b) To apply Itr (fragrance).
   c) To use Miswāk.
   d) To perform marriage."

5. Marriage completes half of one's faith. Sayyidunā Anas
   Ibn Mālik ؓ relates that the Holy Prophet ﷺ said, "When a
   person marries then he fulfils half of his faith, therefore he
   should fear Allāh ﷻ (for the completion) of the remaining
   half." (Mishkāt).

   Completion of one's half of faith implies that mere marriage itself transpires many good qualities within a person
   i.e. prevention from fornication and adultery, prevention
   from evil gazes, striving to become an ideal husband or
   wife, fulfilling each other's rights, striving to become an
   ideal father or mother, maturity, wisdom, God conscious-
   ness, practicing patience, fear of Allāh ﷻ (when carrying
   out one's responsibility) etc.

   ■ Marriage as well as forming an union and a social institu-
   tion between a man and a woman is also an act of continu-
   ous Ibādah (worship). Other forms of worship such as
   Salāh, Fasting, Hajj etc although being amongst the great-
   est forms of worship have restricted times and locations of

being discharged. When the times and places have expired then the completion of Ibādah also comes to an end. On the contrary, the married couple so long as they are in wedlock and abide by all of the Islamic guidelines, are always in the state of Ibādah. This could also include standing, sitting, sleeping, cuddling or even having a sexual relationship. In all these cases a person will be entitled to tremendous rewards from Allāh ﷻ.

The Holy Prophet ﷺ is reported to have said, "Fulfil your desires (in a Halāl way) as this is also Sadaqah (charity)." Upon this the Sahābah ؓ inquired, "How can this be a Sadaqah? If a person is fulfilling his desires then why should he be entitled to reward?" The Holy Prophet ﷺ replied, "If a human being fulfils his desires in a Harām way he will be sinful, similarly if someone fulfils his desires through Halāl measures then he receives reward." (Muslim)

■ To provide expenses for one's family is an act of Sadaqah. The Holy Prophet ﷺ is reported to have said, "Whenever a Muslim spends upon his family (whatever amount) with the aspiration of earning Thawāb (reward) then for him (this is) Sadaqah." (Muslim)

Chapter Two: When should a person marry?

Section One: When to marry?

- When the boy or girl attain the age of puberty (Buloogh) and have the capability of marrying then their marriage should be considered. This includes considering the potential age of marrying, the potential partner etc.

  Sayyidunā Abdullāh Ibn Abbās ﷺ relates that the Holy Prophet ﷺ said, "Whosoever has a child then give him a good name and discipline him (in the Islamic manner), when he attains Buloogh (marriageable age) then he should be married, for if he doesn't marry and commits a sin then the (burden) of sin will be on the parents."

  (Mishkāt)

- Puberty (sexually mature) for a boy is when he experiences a wet dream and semen ejaculates. If he does not experience this until the age of 14 years and 7 months then Islamically he will be considered Bāligh. Once he has attained maturity then all of the obligations of Allāh ﷻ i.e. Salāh, Fasting etc become Fardh upon him.

- A girl will attain Buloogh (maturity) when she experiences menstruation for the first time. Similarly, upon reaching this period all of the obligations of Allāh ﷻ i.e. Salāh, Fasting etc also become Fardh upon her.

16

- When intending to get them married they must be taught the basic guidelines of marriage in relation to it's etiquettes and teachings in Islām i.e. what is marriage all about, the rights of the husband and wife etc.

- There are four categories of Marriage:

1. **Fardh:** When a person has the financial means of supporting a woman and also has the desperate urge of fulfilling his desires with the certainty of becoming a prey to fornication if not married, then marriage will become Fardh upon him.

2. **Wājib:** This is a level below the first category. At this stage the person is financially capable of providing expenses however, there is apprehension (but no certainty) of falling into the sin of fornication then it will become Wājib upon him.

   Note: The status of Fardh is higher than that of Wājib. However, both are necessary to fulfil otherwise a person will be sinful.

3. **Sunnah Muak'kadah:** If a person does not have the urge but has the financial means to marry then it will be Sunnah to marry.

4. **Makrooh:** If a person is unable to support his future wife with the basic necessities or there is apprehension of being unable to fulfil her rights then marrying will be Makrooh.

Inspite of this, if a person was to still have the desperate urge of fulfilling his desires then in this regard the command of the Holy Prophet ﷺ is to frequently fast because this will serve as a protection from sin for him.

Section two: Specific Intentions

- Amongst the etiquettes of marriage is to ensure the sincerity of intentions, because keeping one's motives correct will result in tremendous rewards. The basic intentions are as follows:

1. Performing marriage because it is an act of Sunnah.

2. To save oneself from evil ways, committing a sin and to restrain the Nafs.

3. Through the blessings of marriage, Allāh ﷻ endows us with pious children.

4. A person with a spouse and children will receive more rewards compared to a single person.

5. To increase the Ummah of the Holy Prophet ﷺ.

6. The death of a child will become a means of salvation for the parents in the Hereafter.

Chapter Three: The Etiquettes of choosing a suitable partner

Section One: Searching for the right character

- Choosing a suitable partner is one of the essential aspects of marriage. Meticulous consideration and wisdom must be adopted when selecting a potential partner. When the girl and boy marry then they vow to become life partners hence, much attention is required at this stage so that one can make a wise decision.

- It is amongst the fundamental rights of the child that the parents provide him/her with the basic religious education, an Islamic upbringing and to teach them good manners. As this is imperative upon both parents and especially for the mother, this can only be possible if they search for the right characteristics in their prospective spouse.

  Sayyidunā Abū Hurairah ﷺ relates that the Holy Prophet ﷺ said, "A woman is married for (one of) four reasons; (1) Wealth (2) Beauty (3) Lineage (family nobility) (4) Religion (piety), so choose the pious one or may your hands be covered with dust." (Bukhāri, Muslim)

- Secular education is not an integral characteristic required for the prospective partner in Islām. However, it is highly recommended that one gives preference to religious education after piety or at least to the one who has a basic understanding of Islām.

- It is preferable that the boy marries a girl who is younger than him by age and also who is a virgin. If the girl is older than him or she is a widow or divorced then it is still permissible to marry her.

- The following major points are to be considered when choosing a partner:

a) Their Aqā'id (beliefs) are correct i.e. their beliefs must be in full conformity with the fundamentals of Islām.
b) He/she will not ridicule any of the teachings of the Deen.
c) Have a respectful disposition towards elders and scholars.
d) He/she should be mild tempered towards others i.e. wife, husband, children, elders etc.
e) Show respect to the symbolic signs of Islām i.e. the Masjid, the Ka'bah, the Qur'ān etc.
f) They are expected to fulfil each other's rights and all those who are their subordinates i.e. children etc.
g) Not suffering from any major illnesses resulting in serious problems in the future.
h) Show respect towards elders, treat others with kindness and show compassion towards the young ones.
i) The husband has the necessary means of livelihood to provide Halāl and adequate expenses for his family members.
j) The person is practicing or is willing to try his/her utmost best.
k) Righteousness and good manners.
l) Punctual in carrying out his/her Ibādāt and obligations and have good dealings towards others.

Section Two: Seeing each other during the proposal

- It is highly recommended in Islām that when making a proposal the boy should take a glimpse at the girl after taking consent from the girl's parents before making a firm decision. The Holy Prophet ﷺ encouraged having a glimpse at the prospective partner at the time of proposal.

- Sayyidunā Mugheerah Ibn Shu'bah ؓ relates that I once proposed to a woman then the Holy Prophet ﷺ asked me, "Have you seen her?" I replied, "No." The Holy Prophet ﷺ said, "See her as this will be useful for establishing love between you both." (Ahmad & Tirmizi)

- When the boy at the time of proposal visits the girl then the only parts that are permissible to look at are her face and hands. Anything else is not permissible nor can they touch one another.

- It is prohibited for the boy and girl to date or have any forbidden relationships prior to marrying. Similarly, it is impermissible for a boy and girl to deliberately entertain any imaginary pleasures about each other before marrying.

- In this day and age it is highly recommended that the girl and boy meet and discuss in the presence of the guardians of both parties. The discussion must not be of a casual nature.

- When the boy visits the girl prior to marrying, although there is no harm in discussing their personal matters, both must maintain their modesty. They should not discuss those matters that are irrelevant.

■ It is also recommended that when choosing a suitable partner they should consult either with the scholars or with those who are well acquainted with the background of the girl or boy. The acquaintances could either be friends, colleagues, relatives etc.

When consulting any matter with others then the following points should be borne in mind:

1. Only consult the matter with those who have the full insight.
2. One does not need to consult with anyone regarding those matters that are Fardh (obligatory) or Harām (prohibited), for instance to consult someone to offer Salāh etc. It is obvious that Salāh is Fardh upon every Muslim who is sane and Bāligh.
3. Consult the matter with those who are trustworthy and reliable and with the scholars.
4. It is extremely important that the consultant keeps the matter confidential.
5. When the consultant advises then it is not compulsory (Fardh) for a person to accept that advice when one acknowledges that it may not be appropriate.

■ Once the girl and boy become engaged and agree to marry then it is not permissible for a third party to make a proposal.

Section Three: Istikhārah (to beseech goodness)

- Islām teaches us that after consulting the matter with reliable people then one must also beseech Allāh 🌸 to endow
  goodness in that affair. This is known as Istikhārah. It is
  mentioned in a Hadeeth that the Holy Prophet 🌸 would
  do Istikhārah in almost everything. Although Istikhārah is
  not necessary, it is highly recommended.

- The procedure is that a person after performing Wudhu
  offers two Rak'at Nafl (optional Salāh) with the intention
  of performing Salātul-Istikhārah. Thereafter recite the Istikhārah Du'ā. One may recite whatever Sūrahs he/she wish
  after reciting Sūrah Al-Fātihah. No specific Sūrahs are pre-
  scribed for Salātul-Istikhārah.

- The two Rak'at Salāh cannot be performed during the forbidden and Makrooh times which are after Fajr Salāh, during sunrise, during Zawāl (the zenith), between Asr and
  Maghrib and during sunset. Besides these times, it can be
  performed at any other time.

- It is not necessary to fix a specific time for Salātul-
  Istikhārah. Some people believe that Salātul-Istikhārah
  must be performed immediately after Ishā Salāh, thereafter retire to bed and the bed must be clean otherwise the
  Salātul-Istikhārah will not be accepted and no sign will be
  shown. This self deception has no basis in Islām whatsoev-
  er as it is not a pre-requisite that one has to retire to bed
  instantly and neither keep the bed clean.

■ It is not necessary that one must see a dream straight away nor see a dream at all. Allāh ﷻ can show signs in different ways. For instance, He may inspire a thought in one's heart, or one may consult a reliable person and thus become convinced with their advice. This can also be considered a sign.

■ There is no specific number of days for performing the Salātul-Istikhārah. One may continuously perform it until one becomes convinced. However, a person should not hasten.

Note: Some scholars have fixed a maximum number as seven days.

■ It is permissible to request someone else to offer Salātul-Istikhārah on behalf of oneself.

■ The Du'ā of Istikhārah is as follows:

اَللّٰهُمَّ اِنِّىْ اَسْتَخِيْرُكَ بِعِلْمِكَ وَ اَسْتَقْدِرُكَ بِقُدْرَتِكَ وَ اَسْاَلُكَ مِنْ فَضْلِكَ الْعَظِيْمِ فَاِنَّكَ تَقْدِرُ وَلَا اَقْدِرُ وَتَعْلَمُ وَلَا اَعْلَمُ وَ اَنْتَ عَلَّامُ الْغُيُوْبِ اَللّٰهُمَّ اِنْ كُنْتَ تَعْلَمُ اَنَّ هٰذَا الْاَمْرَ خَيْرٌ لِّىْ فِىْ دِيْنِىْ وَ مَعَاشِىْ وَ عَاقِبَةِ اَمْرِىْ فَاقْدُرْهُ لِىْ وَ يَسِّرْهُ لِىْ ثُمَّ بَارِكْ لِىْ فِيْهِ وَاِنْ كُنْتَ تَعْلَمُ اَنَّ هٰذَا الْاَمْرَ شَرٌّ لِّىْ فِىْ دِيْنِىْ وَ مَعَاشِىْ وَ عَاقِبَةِ اَمْرِىْ فَاصْرِفْهُ عَنِّىْ وَاصْرِفْنِىْ عَنْهُ وَاقْدُرْ لِىَ الْخَيْرَ حَيْثُ كَانَ ثُمَّ اَرْضِنِىْ بِه

Translation: O Allāh! I beseech goodness from You through Your (infinite) knowledge and I seek strength from You through Your (infinite) power and I ask You for Your great favours for surely You

have the power and I don't and You know best whereas I don't and You are the (absolute) Knower of the unseen, O Allāh if in Your knowledge <u>this affair</u> is good for me for my faith, my livelihood and for my Hereafter then decree it for me and make my task easy for me, then bless me therein, however if in Your knowledge <u>this affair</u> is harmful for me in my faith, livelihood and my Hereafter then remove it from me and refrain me from it and decree for me goodness whatever undertaking it may be then make me content with it.

Note: When reaching the underlined points one should remember his/her purpose (in this case think of the prospective partner).

Section Four: Arranged and Love Marriages

- **Arranged Marriage:** Is the concept that the parents or legal guardians of the girl or boy search for a potential partner for their child rather than the boy or girl searching for themselves. This method is not only permissible in Islām but recommended provided it is done with the condition that the parents/legal guardians allow the girl and boy the free will of choice within the Islamic framework, not to pressurise them nor threaten them to marry someone against their wishes.

- **Love Marriage**: Is the concept of where the girl and boy meet one another and after being acquainted with each other, both decide to get married. There are stringent rules

25

in Islām regarding this matter:

1. Islām does not accept the concept of girl friend and boy friend.

2. Islām prohibits all forms of premarital sexual relationships.

3. It is prohibited to date one another.

4. When making a firm decision to marry each other then it is advisable to involve the parents or guardians in order to acquire their blessings.

5. Do Istikhārah.

6. If the parents disagree then they must be informed courteously whilst maintaining their respect. This does not give anyone the licence to ill-treat their parents.

7. Consult the matter with the local scholars.

8. If the boy and girl are not compatible then the parents, guardians have the right to annul the marriage. However, if they are compatible then the parents/guardians cannot object. This will be discussed in the chapter of Kafā'at In-shā-Allāh.

Chapter Four: Kafā'at or Kuf'u (Compatibility)

Definition:

The suitability of the boy and girl who propose to each other for marriage purpose is known as Kafā'at.

- Islamically, compatibility between the boy and girl is very important. When compatibility is found then marriage should not be delayed. The Holy Prophet ﷺ said, "O Ali! there are three things which you must not delay; Salāh when it comes, a funeral when it is ready and a spouse when a suitable match is found." (Tirmizi)

- Not searching for a suitable partner can inevitably result in a major marriage breakdown. Hence when searching for a prospective partner, it is necessary to ensure that the girl and boy are suitable for one another.

- Compatibility is usually considered from the girl's side. There is no harm if the boy is of a higher status than the girl. But if the girl is more highly professional than the boy then this would not be considered Kafā'at. If the boy is wealthy or of a professional calibre compared to the girl then this will be considered Kafā'at.

- If compatibility does not exist between the boy and girl then the guardians have the full authority to demand a separation between the boy and the girl. This is because the Shari'ah has considered compatibility to be the sole right of the parents/legal guardians. Where compatibility exists then the guardians have no authority to intervene with the marriage and neither can they demand a separation between them.

Note: The most appropriate method with regards to incompatibility between the married couple (or for any other problems) is to refer the case to a Shar'ee Panchayit (an Islamic Shar'ee council governed by scholars).

- In the case where compatibility does not exist between the couple, the marriage will be left pending with the consent of the guardians, if they accept the marriage then it will be valid otherwise not.

- Compatibility is mainly considered in four major aspects:
  1. Nasab (family lineage)
  2. Occupation
  3. Wealth
  4. Religion and righteousness

1. Nasab (family lineage)

- Nasab implies compatibility in family nobility, lineage and family background.

- Islamically, the family lineage is always associated to the father's side and not to the mother's, for instance if the father is a Sayyid and the mother is not then the child will be considered as a Sayyid. However, if the mother is a Sayyid and the father is not then the child will not be a Sayyid.

■ Sayyid are those people who are from the descendants of Sayyidah Fātimah 👑 and from Sayyidunā Hasan 👑 and Sayyidunā Husain 👑.

Note: Although the family lineage is linked to the father's side, there is an exemption in the case of Sayyidah Fātimah 👑 because the Holy Prophet 👑 had explicitly stated that my generation is from Sayyidah Fātimah's 👑 descendants.

■ Gujrati, Pakistani, Bangladeshi, Pathān, Chachi, Punjabi are all compatible with one another i.e. if a Pathān was to marry a Gujrati or a Bangladeshi was to marry a Pakistani or a Bangladeshi was to marry a Guajrati or a Chachi then they are all considered compatible with one another.

■ Choudry, Qasbi, Surti, Baroochi, Sylheti, Dhakai etc. are all compatible to one another.

■ If the girl belongs to a noble background whereas the boy is from a poor background then compatibility would be considered.

2. Occupation

■ Compatibility in terms of occupation is intangible; it is difficult to be precise about which occupation is compatible with another due to the variation of customs, people's common perception at the time and the geographical location. Therefore, the Fuqahā (Muslim jurists) have stated a principle in the books of Fiqh that according to the time and location whichever jobs are commonly considered to be compatible with one another then they will be considered compatible otherwise not.

- A person working as a dustbin man is not commonly considered to be compatible with a woman who is working in a professional job. Therefore there would be no compatibility between them from an occupational point of view.

- If a person working in a factory, restaurant, takeaway, a taxi driver, mechanic etc intends to marry a woman who is highly educated and works in a professional job, then if this is commonly considered compatible with one another then they will be compatible otherwise not.

3. Wealth

- Compatibility in terms of wealth means that a poor and penniless man is not a suitable match with a woman who is wealthy and rich.

- If a man who is not wealthy but is able to pay the Mahr (dowry) and able to provide adequate expenses for the woman who comes from a richer background then this would be considered compatible. It is not necessary for the man to be equally as rich as the woman.

4. Religion and Piety

- Religion means the couple being religious and piety means they practice and adhere to the teachings of Islām.

Note: There is an exemption with regards to men marrying the Ahl-e-Kitāb (the people of the Book) because Allāh ﷻ has permitted this in the Holy Qur'ān. This will be discussed in detail in the chapter of Muharramāt, Inshā-Allāh.

- A religious woman who prays her five daily prayers, observes the Hijāb etc is not compatible with a man who is involved in open sin and does not practice at all.

- There is no harm if the boy is more adherent to the Islamic principles than the girl as long as she is trying her utmost best.

- A man being irreligious is of three categories:

  1. The man being a Non-Muslim whether he is a Christian, Jew, an idolater or an atheist. This type of marriage with a Muslim woman would not be permissible and if done then they will be committing sin throughout their married life.

  2. A woman is a Sunni and the man is affiliated to a group or sect that harbour corrupt Aqā'id (beliefs) then this marriage would also be impermissible. Similarly if the man is a Muslim and a woman harbours corrupt Aqā'id then the marriage will not be valid.

  3. If a man is irreligious and involved in open sins whilst the woman is pious then this would not be considered as Kafā'at.

Miscellaneous

- An insane woman is not compatible with a sane man and neither is an insane man compatible with a sane woman.

- Compatibility in terms of age is also considered. Hence, if an old man was to marry a very young girl or if the matter was visa-versa then this would be incompatible.

Chapter Five: The Legal Guardian

Section One: The sequence of priority to become the Legal Guardian

- Islamically the person who has the legal right to give the girl and the boy away in marriage is known as the **Legal Guardian**.

- The sequence of precedence to be a legal guardian is as follows:

  First the father - If not then the paternal grandfather - If there are no paternal grandfathers then the elder brother - then the paternal step brother. If any male relatives do not exist then the mother will become the legal guardian – then the maternal grandfather – then the paternal grandmother – then the maternal grandmother.

- A non-Muslim, a child and an insane person cannot become the legal guardian of the boy or girl. In such a case, the authority of guardianship will be transferred to the next person in the sequence mentioned above.

Section Two: The method of consulting the girl and the prohibition of forced marriage

- When a free and sane girl becomes Bāligh (sexually mature and begins to menstruate) then it is compulsory in

Islām to obtain her consent when selecting a suitable partner for her. It is not permissible for any of the legal guardians to marry the girl (or boy) to someone by force. Sayyidunā Abū Hurairah 🕮 relates that the Holy Prophet 🕮
said, "A matron (a woman who was previously married)
should not be married off unless she is consulted and a
virgin girl should not be married off unless permission is
sought (from her)." They inquired, "O Messenger of Allāh
🕮 how should her granting permission be?" He said,
"When she remains silent (in agreement)."

(Bukhāri, Muslim)

Sayyidunā Abdullāh Ibn Abbās 🕮 relates, "A virgin girl
once came to the Holy Prophet 🕮 and stated (in the form
of complaining) that her father married her off (to someone) whilst she was displeased. The Holy Prophet 🕮 gave
her the choice (either remain with her husband or to annul
the marriage)." (Abū Dāwood)

- From the aforementioned Ahādeeth, it can be deduced
  that if a woman is forcefully married to someone against
  her wishes and results in further problems in the marriage, then she is permitted to approach an Islamic judge
  (or a Shar'ee council governed by scholars) and demand a
  separation.

- The simplest method would be that when the girl becomes
  physically and mentally prepared to marry and reaches
  the appropriate age, the legal guardians should begin to
  search for a potential partner for her within the guidelines
  of the Islamic principles. The family could either search

within their close or distant relatives or outside the family but Deen and character should always be given prefer- ence. If they find a potential match for the girl (or boy) then they must inform the matter to her in full details with honesty. After confiding in her then allow them to see each other but in the presence of the parents or legal guardians of both parties. She must be given the freedom to ponder over the matter and to do Istikhārah. If she grants permission then take the matter further but if she declines then search for another potential partner.

- When the legal guardian seeks permission from the girl who is a virgin and she either remains silent, laughs, smiles or sheds tears (implying agreement) then all this will be classed as her granting permission. However, if she clearly refuses then do not marry her to that person.

- If a matron girl is sought permission then it is necessary for her to express her permission verbally. Remaining si- lent or shedding tears will not be sufficient.

- It is extremely important that the parents or legal guardi- ans allow the girl and boy to make their own choice and decide for themselves as long as their decision does not conflict with Islām.

- If a girl and boy marry in the presence of two male wit- nesses or one male and two female witnesses without in- forming or obtaining the consent from the legal guardian then the marriage would legally be valid. However, this method is highly detestable, if it was practiced then such marriage will be deprived of blessings.

- According to the Hanafi Fiqh the above marriage will still be legally valid. Nevertheless, in this day and age many people misuse this Mas'alah and employ it in the wrong way. Therefore in order to prevent further problems it is highly suggested that the legal guardian is always present at the time of the marriage.

- If a girl and boy marry someone of their choice then the parents/guardian are not permitted to reject the marriage nor can they demand a separation from an Islamic judge (or a Shar'ee council governed by scholars) as long as there is compatibility between them. But if the boy is not compatible with the girl then the parents/guardian have the authority to intervene and demand a separation.

- Inspite the fact that Islām has given the girl and boy the right to marry the person of their choice, it would be appropriate that the choice be in conjunction with their parents wishes in order to acquire their blessings. If one disapproves of the parent's choice then the parents must be informed politely and clearly whilst maintaining their respect. This does not give anyone the licence to ill-treat them or use any words of contempt against them.

- If the guardian gives the girl away in marriage without her consent and she is Bāligh, free and a sane girl then the marriage will be left pending upon her consent; if she permits then the marriage will be valid otherwise not. If after getting her married without her consent she was informed and she remained silent or gave such an impression that indicates towards her granting permission then the marriage will be valid. If she clearly refuses then the marriage will be invalid.

Section Three: Miscellaneous

- When informing the girl or the boy about their potential match then it is necessary to give the following basic information:

  1. Full Name
  2. Place of residence
  3. Specify any disabilities
  4. Occupation
  5. Personality which includes manners.
  6. Level of Islamic Knowledge
  7. Practicing or trying their level best
  8. Family

- In the presence of the legal guardian if someone else sought permission from a virgin girl then it would be necessary for her to express her permission verbally.

- If the guardian lives far away to the extent that if they wait to consult the matter with him then it will cause delay resulting in further problems. In such extreme circumstances it would be permissible for the next closest guardian to arrange the marriage for the girl. For instance, if the father is far away and it is difficult to obtain his consent then the paternal grandfather is allowed to marry the girl and if he is unapproachable due to circumstances then the elder brother.

- However, in the presence of the legal guardian who is approachable, it would not be permissible for another person to get the girl married for instance; if the father is available then the grandfather or brother will not be the legal guardian nor do they have the authority to get the girl married.

- All the injunctions that pertain to the girl are also applicable to the boy, except that when obtaining permission from the boy he must express it verbally; remaining silent will be insufficient.

Chapter Six: Muharramāt

Section one: Those relatives to whom marriage is not permissible

Definition: Muharramāt are those relatives to whom marriage is permanently forbidden. Such relatives are usually referred to as Mahram and Hijāb is not observed from such people. Allāh ﷻ has listed in Sūrah An-Nisā (4:23) those relatives to whom marriage is prohibited. They are as follows:

■ It is totally and eternally forbidden for a man to marry his mother, sister, daughter, maternal and paternal grandparents all the way above and similarly grandchildren all the way down.

■ It is not permissible for a man to marry his maternal and paternal aunties and nieces from brother's or sister's side.

■ The similar case is with a woman i.e. she is not allowed to marry her father, brother, son, uncle; paternal or maternal, nephews either from brothers or sisters, grandparents from both parents, the sons of nephews and grandchildren all the way down.

■ Whilst a man is in wedlock to a woman, it is impermissible for him to marry his wife's sister. However, if he divorced her or she passed away then it would be permissible for him to marry her sister. But in the case of divorce he can only marry his wife's sister once she has completed her Iddah (waiting period).

■ It is not permissible for a man to join two sisters in his wedlock and neither is it permissible for him to bring two such women in his wedlock between whom if one of them from both sides was supposedly a man then marriage would not be permissible between them. For instance, Zaid intends to marry Zainab and Fātimah, however Fāti-mah is the aunty of Zainab. If Zainab was supposedly a man then it would not be permissible for a nephew to marry his aunt. Similarly, if Fātimah was supposedly a man then it would not be permissible for a man to marry his own niece. Therefore, it would not be permissible for Zaid to bring Fātimah and Zainab into his wedlock togeth-er.

■ Fostering another person's child does not make him/her a real son or daughter. They are still Ghair-Mahram and does not make this child a real biological brother or sister hence it would be permissible to marry them.

■ A woman whilst in wedlock to a man is not permitted to marry anyone else. Once she is divorced from her hus-band or he passed away and she has completed her Iddat then she is permitted to marry someone else.

Section Two: Hurmat-e-Radhā'ah (prohibited through breastfeeding)

■ A woman breast feeding an infant (other than her own child) will become the suckling mother of that infant. Sim-ilarly, her husband will become the suckling father of that infant and also her sons and daughters become the suckling brothers and sisters of that suckled child. Likewise the woman's and the man's brothers, sisters and parents will become the suckling uncles, aunts and grandparents of that child.

- All those relatives that are prohibited to marry through blood relationship are also prohibited through a breast feeding relationship. This is known as Hurmat-e-Radhā'ah. However, if the breast milk was mixed with another liquid, for instance water then the majority quantity will be taken into account; if the breast milk is more than the water then Hurmat-e-Radā'ah will be established otherwise not.

Section Three: Hurmat-e-Musāharat

- If a man had intercourse with a woman whether inside or outside of wedlock then it becomes eternally prohibited upon him to marry any of her ascendants i.e. mother and grandmother all the way above and her descendants i.e. daughters and granddaughters all the way down. Similarly, if a woman had intercourse with a man whether inside or outside of wedlock, then his father and grand-father all the way above and son and grandsons all the way down become prohibited upon her to marry. This is known as Hurmat-e-Musāharat.

- When the girl and boy marry, it now becomes eternally prohibited for the boy to marry his mother in-law and likewise the girl to marry her father in-law irrespective of whether they had intercourse or not. Merely through wedlock it becomes eternally unlawful to marry mother in-laws and father in-laws.

41

- If a man married such a woman who already has a daughter from a previous husband and subsequently this second husband before having an intimate relationship with her, divorced her or she passed away then it would be permissible for him to marry her daughter. It would not matter whether the girl is in his custody or not. However, if the man divorced her or she passed away after having an intimate relationship then it would not be permissible for him to marry her daughter.

- The above case will not apply to a woman, hence if a woman marries a man who already has a son from a previous wife and later on, he either dies or divorced her then she is not permitted to marry his son whether they had intercourse or not. In this regard, mere wedlock prohibits her to marry her ex-husband's son/s .

- If the boy's father was to have more than one wife then it would not be permissible for him to marry any of his stepmother/s.

Section Four: Marrying those of other faiths

- It is not permissible for a Muslim man or woman to marry a polytheist, atheist, apostate or a Zindeeq. If done then the marriage will not be valid.

Note: Zindeeq is that person who practices Islām externally, but also harbours such beliefs that takes him out of the fold of Islām.

- It is not permissible for a woman to marry an Ahle-Kitāb

(Jew or Christian) man, however it will be permissible for a Muslim male to marry an Ahle-Kitāb woman.

Note: An Ahle-Kitāb refers to those Jews and Christians who strictly adhere and practice the fundamental teachings of their scriptures and are not involved in any kind of shameless and obscene practices.

- If either of the non-Muslim married couple embrace Islām then merely embracing Islām will not invalidate the marriage. Islām should be presented to the spouse. If he/she accepts Islām then the marriage will remain intact but if he/she refuses then the marriage will automatically break.

- If either of them embrace Islām whilst the other is still considering it, then although the marriage will still remain intact they are not permitted to have intercourse.

- If a woman accepts Islām but her husband refuses then they will be separated and this separation will be Talāq-e-Bā'in. Hence she must observe her required Iddah. However if the husband accepts Islām but his wife refuses then this separation will not be classed as a Talāq.

- If the husband and wife accept Islām together then their marriage will remain intact even though their marriage was performed differently to that of Islām.

Chapter Seven: How to perform the Marriage

■ It is Sunnah that the marriage is performed in the Masjid. It is recommended that the marriage is conducted by a scholar or an Imām.

■ It is preferable to offer general Naseehat (advice) before commencing the marriage.

■ The advice should constitute the following main points:
  1. The importance of marriage.
  2. Its benefits.
  3. To vow to live together as a married couple.
  4. Explain the importance of fulfilling the rights of each other.
  5. Refer to the reliable scholars to seek Islamic guidelines at times of difficulties.

■ If the marriage is conducted in a house, hall etc then it will be permissible.

■ There are two Fardh (obligations) acts at the time of performing the marriage without which the marriage will Islamically not be valid.

1. **Ijāb and Qabool:** This means that at the time of performing the marriage there should be categorical approval from both parties. For instance when the Imām addresses the girl or her representative, "Have you accepted such and such man in your marriage?" They clearly reply, "Yes,

I have accepted" or "I have accepted to give such and such girl in the marriage of such and such person." The similar case is with the boy.

2. **Witnesses:** The witnesses should be either two males or one male and two females. The qualities of the witnesses should be Muslims, sane and Bāligh.

Note: It is preferable that the witnesses be honest, upright and practicing although this is not legally necessary.

Section One: Method

■ The simplest method of performing marriage is as follows:

1. Appoint an Imām, scholar or any other reliable person who is aware of the basic Masā'il of how to perform the marriage.
2. The minimum requirement of people to be present in the ceremony of marriage is the groom (or his representative), the bride (or her representative), reliable witnesses; either two males or one male and two females and the legal guardian.
3. The performer will recite the Masnoon Khutbah (sermon) followed by the recitation of three verses of the Qur'ān; the first from Sūrah Al-Imrān (verse 102), the second from Sūrah An-Nisā (verse 1) and the third from Sūrah Al-Ahzāb (verse 70-71). This will then be followed by quoting a few Ahādeeth pertaining to marriage.
4. Thereafter the performer will address the bride or the representative of the bride in the form of a question i.e. "Do

you accept to marry such and such person" or anything similar to that effect. If the bride or the representative replies in the affirmative then the performer will now address the groom in a similar manner. Once he has replied in the affirmative the marriage will be complete.

Section Two: Miscellaneous

- The marriage ceremony should be publicised amongst people as much as possible. It is undesirable to conduct a marriage ceremony in secrecy.

- It is highly recommended (but not compulsory) that prior to performing the marriage a final consent is sought from the girl and boy to avoid further predicaments.

- When deciding to perform the marriage by an Imām or scholar etc then the representative of the girl should be present in the gathering rather than the girl due to the laws of Hijāb. However, if the girl is present in the gathering and speaks on her own behalf and the two main conditions of marriage are fulfilled then the marriage will still be valid.

- It is Masnoon to make a short Du'ā collectively after performing the marriage. It is Sunnah for the performer to recite the following Masnoon Du'ā:

بَارَكَ اللهُ كَكَ وَبَارَكَ عَلَيْكُمَا وَ جَمَعَ بَيْنَكُمَا بِالْخَيْرِ

Trans: May Allāh ﷻ bless you and (also) shower His Blessings over you both and join goodness between you both.

46

Chapter Eight: Mahr (Dowry)

Section One: The ruling of Mahr

- Allāh ﷻ states in the Holy Qur'ān, "And give to the women (whom you marry) their dowry with good heart." (4:4)

  "So with those amongst whom you have gained pleasure from, then give them their required due." (4:24)

- The money that is necessary for the groom to give to the bride in exchange of retaining her in his wedlock is called the Mahr. The bride has the full right over the Mahr and she can demand it whenever she wishes and utilise it however she wishes within the parameters of the Islamic guidelines.

- It is compulsory (Wājib) upon the groom to give the Mahr to the bride irrespective of whether it was mentioned during the marriage ceremony or not. It is not compulsory to state the amount of Mahr during the performance of marriage although it is preferable to do so.

- If someone marries with the condition of not giving Mahr to the bride, it is still compulsory upon the groom to give Mahr to her.

- The amount of Mahr which is agreed by both parties is known as Mahr-e-Musamma (stipulated dowry). If the Mahr was not fixed for the bride then the ruling is that the Mahr which was fixed for the bride's sister/s or aunt at their wedding, will be stipulated for the bride. Such Mahr is known as Mahr-e-Mithl (this will be discussed in detail later on in this chapter Inshā-Allāh).

- The minimum requisite amount of Mahr to be fixed is ten Dirhams. Although there is no maximum limit, the amount agreed should be reasonable to avoid difficulty and extravagance.

- It is Sunnah to stipulate Mahr-e-Fātimi as a dowry for the bride. Mahr-e-Fātimi is that dowry which the Holy Prophet ﷺ stipulated for his daughter, Sayyidah Fātimah ﷺ. The amount of dowry that he fixed was 500 Dirhams.

- After marriage if the husband and wife had intimate relations with one another or they did not but Khalwat-e-Saheehah took place (i.e. to remain secluded for such a length of time and in a place that would not Islamically nor medically prevent them from having intercourse) and furthermore, the Mahr was fixed (i.e. Mahr-e-Musamma) then it is compulsory for the husband to give the full amount of Mahr to his wife. However, if the husband divorced his wife immediately after marriage and neither did they have intimate relations nor did Khalwat-e-Saheehah take place then the wife will be entitled to half of the Mahr.

- Khalwat-e-Saheehah and intercourse both hold the same injunction in Mahr. The key principle to remember is if Khalwat-e-Saheehah or intimate relations take place then the bride will be entitled to the full amount of Mahr, however if neither of the two take place and the husband divorced his wife then she will only be eligible to half of the fixed Mahr.

- If after marriage either of them passed away then the wife (or her legal guardian if she passed away) will be entitled to the full amount of Mahr whether Khalwat-e-Saheehah or intimate relations occurred or not. This is an exception to the general rule.

- If mere seclusion took place (but no intimate relationship) whilst either of them was severely ill such that they were unable to have intercourse, or at a time or place where Islām disallows intercourse for instance; the woman is menstruating, in the state of fasting during the month of Ramadhān (not including the other types of fast), whilst in Ihrām or in the Masjid then it will not be classed as Khalwat-e-Saheehah. Therefore, if the husband after such seclusion instantly divorces his wife then she will be entitled to half of the Mahr only.

- All of the above mentioned scenarios refer to that type of Mahr which has been stipulated (Mahr-e-Musamma). If the Mahr was not fixed at all during the contract of marriage and the husband and wife either had intimate relations or Khalwat-e-Saheehah took place and thereafter he divorced her then the wife will be entitled to the full amount of Mahr-e-Mithl.

- In the case of Mahr-e-Mithl, if the husband divorced his wife prior to intercourse or Khalwat-e-Saheehah then the wife will be entitled to Mut'a; which means giving her a reasonable quality suit. Half of the Mahr-e-Mithl will not be given as in the case of Mahr-e-Musamma.

- If either of them passed away, then the wife will still be entitled to the entire Mahr-e-Mithl whether Khalwat-e-Saheehah or intercourse took place or not.

- If during the contract of marriage, the Mahr was not agreed, then subsequently the husband and wife agreed upon a fixed Mahr then the wife will be entitled to whatever amount was agreed. However, if the husband divorced her prior to Khalwat-e-Saheehah or intercourse then the wife will be entitled to a Mut'a (a reasonable quality suit).

- If £100 Mahr was initially fixed, thereafter the husband out of generosity supplemented it by another £100 on top, now it becomes compulsory for the husband to give £200 to the bride. If he refuses then he will become sinful. However, if the husband divorced his wife before intercourse or Khalwat-e-Saheehah then she will only be eligible to that half of the amount of Mahr which was initially stipulated i.e. she will only receive £50.

- If the bride wishes to either remit some portion or the entire Mahr then that is her right of choice. It is a common trend and belief that the legal guardian of the bride are the rightful owners of the Mahr. This is false and has no basis in Islām, however if the bride wants to give it to her legal guardian then she may do so.

- If the husband divorced his wife and he had already paid her the Mahr then he is not permitted to reclaim the Mahr back from her, neither would it be permissible for him to threaten his wife to either reduce or forgo the Mahr. This is strictly forbidden in Islām and by doing so he will be very sinful.

- Besides money, any item or object that is legitimate for a Muslim to use can also be agreed and fixed as a Mahr for instance a house, car etc. Whatever is not permissible for a Muslim to use, cannot be agreed as a Mahr for instance alcohol, swine etc. In such a case the marriage will be valid but Mahr-e-Mithl will become compulsory and not the forbidden item.

Section two: Mahr-e-Mithl

- If during the contract of the marriage the dowry was not stipulated for the bride and nor was it thereafter, or the Mahr that has been fixed is a forbidden item for instance alcohol, swine etc then Mahr-e-Mithl becomes necessary for her.

- Mahr-e-Mithl means a comparable amount of Mahr that was given to a girl of the bride's relative from her father's lineage. Such relatives include sister, paternal aunt and paternal cousin sister.

- The Mahr of the bride's mother will not be considered unless if she was previously the paternal relative of the bride's father, only then her Mahr will be considered. For instance before she married Zaid, she was his paternal cousin sister.

- The basic qualities for the comparison of such relatives include:
  1. Age
  2. Beauty
  3. Whether her marriage took place when she was a virgin or not
  4. Understanding
  5. Wealth

If the aforementioned qualities are matching or closely matching to the bride then such a relative's Mahr that was fixed during her marriage will likewise be fixed for the bride.

Section Three: Jahaiz (Gifts)

- Jahaiz is a supplementary gift that is usually given to the couple from the bride's side. The Jahaiz should be simple and devoid of any extravagance.

- The Jahaiz that the Messenger of Allāh 🕮 gave to his beloved daughter, Sayyidah Fātimah 🕮 was a silver bracelet, two Yemeni sheets, four mattresses, one blanket, one pillow, one cup, one hand grinding mill, one bedstead, a small water skin and a leather pitcher (similar to a jug).

- Unlike Mahr, Jahaiz is not compulsory.

- It is not permissible for the bridegroom or his family to demand any gifts, money etc from the bride's side as they are not obliged to do so. However, if they out of affection and courteousness present a gift to the groom without him demanding it then it will be permissible.

- Nowadays, gifts given in the name of Jahaiz are not classed as Jahaiz due to the following reasons:
  1. People have become extravagant in giving gifts.
  2. People are obliged and pressured to give gifts which is totally wrong.
  3. At times the groom also demands gifts from others whereas he is not permitted to do so.
  4. It has become a compulsory act and by not complying, others will criticise which is totally wrong.
  5. At times the gift that is given is not permissible for instance, gold rings and chain for men etc.
  6. People have started to compete in giving gifts.

Therefore, it would be preferable to avoid rendering gifts unless one is adamant that the Jahaiz is devoid of the aforementioned motives, only then it will be permissible.

Note: Some scholars are of the opinion that there is no such thing as Jahaiz (gifts) as Jahaiz is derived from the Arabic word 'jahaz' which literally means to prepare basic necessities. The gifts that the Holy Prophet ﷺ gave to Sayyidah Fātimah ؓ were in reality the basic necessities that he provided on behalf of Sayyidunā Ali ؓ.

Chapter Nine: Waleemah and Rukhsati (Departure)

Section One: The ruling and guidelines of Waleemah

- The marriage feast that is held after the marriage ceremony for commemorating the union of a newly wedded couple whereby the family, relatives and friends are invited to partake in a feast is called the Waleemah.

- Waleemah is an outward expression of gratitude and happiness. It is an effective means of publicity for the marriage because the Holy Prophet ﷺ emphasised that the marriage should be publicised.

- Waleemah is Sunnah and it was the practice of the Holy Prophet ﷺ to conduct a simple Waleemah ceremony after the marriage. Sayyidunā Anas ؓ relates that the Holy Prophet ﷺ performed the Waleemah when he married Zainab Bint Jahash ؓ. He fed the people with bread and meat. (Bukhāri)

  Sayyidunā Anas ؓ relates that the Holy Prophet ﷺ did not perform Waleemah of any of his wives similar to that of Zainab's ؓ Waleemah. He performed the Waleemah with a goat (i.e. slaughtered a goat and fed the people).
  (Bukhāri ,Muslim)

Note: This Hadeeth refers to the simplicity of the Holy Prophet's ﷺ Waleemah ceremony of his other wives. For instance, it is stated in Bukhāri and Muslim that when the Holy

Prophet ﷺ married Sayyidah Safiyyah ﷺ, he performed a Waleemah merely on dates, cheese and butter. The table cloth was devoid of any meat.

- Although the Waleemah is Sunnah, it is highly emphasised to accept the invitation of a Waleemah. Sayyidunā Abdullāh Ibn Umar ﷺ relates that the Holy Prophet ﷺ said, "If anyone amongst you is invited to a Waleemah feast then he must attend it." (Bukhāri, Muslim)

- There are certain exceptions where attending a Waleemah feast is not permissible:

    1. Music
    2. Singing and dancing
    3. Intermingling of men and women
    4. The food served is Harām or extremely doubtful
    5. Photographs and filming
    6. Any un-Islamic practices, sins or innovations are taking place

Note: Due to the prevalence of the aforementioned practices in modern times, it is advisable that a person primarily enquires before attending any Waleemah ceremony.

- The groom or his guardian are responsible for the expenditure of the Waleemah ceremony. The bride or her guardian are not responsible for anything. However, if they wish to contribute voluntarily then that will be their courteous act.

- It is not permissible to become extravagant when spending on the Waleemah ceremony. Sayyidah Ā'ishah ﷺ relates that the Holy Prophet ﷺ said, "The most blessed marriage is wherein there is the least expenditure."

(Baihaqi)

- Nowadays people compete with one another in celebrating the Waleemah. This is not permissible, the simpler the marriage the more blessings there will be Inshā-Allāh.

- The Waleemah should be devoid of excessive decorations as this becomes a means of pride and arrogance which are not permitted in Islām.

- It is difficult to determine simplicity as traditions and local customs vary from time to time. Hence when conducting a Waleemah, the following points must be borne in mind:

  1. No sins, un-Islamic acts or innovation take place.
  2. The marriage is performed in accordance with Islamic guidelines (refer to Ch.7 - How to Perform Marriage).
  3. The cost and expenditure is not spent on unnecessary or un-Islamic things like fireworks etc.
  4. Adequate money is spent to fulfil the basic necessities.

- It is not necessary to hire a hall for the Waleemah ceremony. Even inviting guests at one's own residence will be sufficient for the fulfilment of a Sunnah Waleemah. This was the practice of the Holy Prophet ﷺ when he got married to Sayyidah Zainab Bint Jahash ﷺ , he invited all the guests to his house. However, if so many guests are invited that the residence would not be sufficient to accommodate all of them then a reasonable standard hall may be hired.

- It is a common belief and practice that it is compulsory that two days of Waleemah must be held; one from the bride's side and the other from the groom's side. This has no basis in the Shari'ah as the responsibility of the expenditure is on the shoulders of the groom or his guardians. One day of Waleemah is sufficient for the Sunnah to be fulfilled.

- The Waleemah ceremony should be conducted either on the same day or the following day of the marriage. Sayyidunā Anas ﷺ relates that when the Holy Prophet ﷺ married Zainab Bint Jahash ﷺ , then he conducted the Waleemah the following day. (Baihaqi)

- If one day of Waleemah is not enough to feed all the guests then due to necessity, the Waleemah can be held for two or three consecutive days. After the third day the Waleemah should not be continued.

- The Sunnah is to hold the Waleemah within seven days after the marriage. After seven days the marriage feast that is held will not be classed as the Sunnah Waleemah but will be considered merely a Da'wat (normal invitation).

- It is only permissible to give gifts and money to the bride and groom if it is not regarded as compulsory, a Shar'ee obligation nor is a person pressured by others. If that is the case then it is not permissible. Giving a gift or Hadyah is Mustahab (desirable) and encouraged in Islām when it is given out of love and affection at anytime or any occasion. Therefore, it is incorrect to restrict gifts to specific times, occasions or to consider it compulsory.

Section Two: Rukhsati (Departure)

- The time when the girl after the marriage departs from her home to permanently reside with her husband is usually known as Rukhsati.

- Rukhsati should be done instantly after the marriage. It is wrong to delay the Rukhsati of the girl unless there are dire circumstances.

- The Rukhsati can take place either before or after the Waleemah.

- It is commonly practiced in certain families that a few days after the Rukhsati, it is necessary that the girl returns to her parent's house for a few nights and then her mother in-law goes over to collect her. This has absolutely no basis in the Shari'ah and to consider it an integral practice of the Rukhsati is a grave sin.

- Upon arriving at the husband's residence, they should greet each other with Salām and thereafter the husband should place his right hand on her hair towards the forehead and recite the following Du'ā;

اَللّٰهُمَّ اِنِّیۡ اَسۡئَلُكَ خَیۡرَهَا وَ خَیۡرَ مَا جَبَلۡتَهَا عَلَیۡهِ وَ اَعُوۡذُ بِكَ مِنۡ شَرِّهَا وَ شَرِّ مَا جَبَلۡتَهَا عَلَیۡهِ

Translation: O Allāh! Verily I ask You her goodness and that goodness upon which You have created her and I seek Your protection from her evil and from that evil upon which You have created her. (Abū Dāwood)

- It is extremely important that the girl and boy have a good impression upon one another when meeting each other for the first time and not hasten into things.

Chapter Ten: Etiquettes of an Intimate Relationship between the Husband and Wife

- Allāh ﷻ states in the Holy Qur'ān, "So now you can have sexual intimacy with them and seek what Allāh has destined for you (i.e. children)." (2:187)

  "Your women are a tillage for you (to cultivate) so come to your tillage from wherever you wish." (2:223)

  Allāh ﷻ has made lawful for mankind to derive sexual pleasure from their spouses. As Islām is a complete way of life, it has also set down regulations and guidelines for the couple pertaining to an intimate relationship. Hence it is necessary to understand them very well. It is very unfortunate that this topic is overlooked by many people.

- Intimate relations with one's spouse is a meritorious act in Islām to the extent that it is mentioned in a Hadeeth that it is an act of charity.

- Intimate relations is the right of the husband and the wife. It is necessary that the couple fulfil each other's desires when the need arises otherwise both of them will be sinful for neglecting each other's right.

- Although there is no stipulation or restriction on how often the couple should engage in intimate relations but as a medical perspective it is recommended to consummate at least once a week.

■ The Fuqahā (Islamic Jurists) have stated that it is compulsory for a man to have intimate relations with his wife at least once in four months otherwise he will become very sinful.

Section One: Preparation

■ Before the couple consummate, they should ensure the following etiquettes:

1. Total privacy - no third person should be present in the same room not even an animal or a child who has reached the age of understanding and comprehends what is taking place in front of them. Sayyidunā Abdullāh Ibn Umar ؓ would (as a precaution) remove a breast feeding child from the room before consummating.

2. Ensure the doors are locked and the curtains drawn completely to prevent anyone from watching.

3. To conceal the acts of intimacy. It is a sinful act for the couple to make any unnecessary noise during intimacy.

4. To cover themselves with a sheet, blanket etc.

5. Not to talk excessively during consummation.

6. It is totally unlawful for a man with two (or more) wives to consummate with both of them simultaneously even if the wives give the consent.

7. To cover up the Holy Qur'ān or to put it away.

8. Recite the following Du'ā when intending to consummate (to be recited by the husband and wife).

بِسُمِ اللهِ اَللّٰهُمَّ جَنِّبْنَا الشَّيْطَانَ وَجَنِّبِ الشَّيْطَانَ مَا رَزَقْتَنَا

Translation: In the name of Allāh, O Allāh! Protect us from the Shaytān and protect what You grant us (i.e. the coming offspring) from the Shaytān. (Bukhāri, Muslim)

■ Before consummating, the couple should adorn themselves by:

1. Applying Itr (perfume).
2. Removing unwanted pubic hair and the hair from under the armpits. A woman is permitted to remove the hair from her arms, legs and the rest of the body to adorn herself for her husband.
3. Removing unpleasant body odours and bad breath.
4. Refreshing oneself by performing Ghusl or Wudhu.
5. Appearing appealing and attractive for one another.
6. Good treatment and seduction.
7. Psychological preparation.

■ To foreplay with one another before and during consummation is very important and encouraged in Islām. This will enable the increase of passion for one another. For instance, hugging, cuddling, kissing, sucking, massaging, fondling with each other's genitals, etc.

■ It is permissible for the couple to be totally unclothed when consummating.

■ It is permissible for the husband to masturbate with the hand of his wife and similarly the wife to masturbate with her husband's hand. This is usually referred to as mutual masturbation. Self-masturbation is totally prohibited.

Section Two: Engaging in intercourse and the permitted and prohibited acts

- The Shari'ah has not specified any particular time of the day or night when the couple should engage in intimate relations. However the following points are some suggestions and preferred times:

  1. At a time when both are relaxed and a temperamental balance exists.
  2. During the last portion of the night.
  3. The night that precedes Friday or on Friday.

- In general, Islām grants the couple the permission to choose whatever sexual position they feel comfortable with as long as it is restricted to vaginal sex only. Any position that does not involve vaginal sex (i.e. anal sex) is prohibited.

- The Sunnah and the natural position is for the husband to lie on top of his wife whilst she lies on her back with her legs spread. The husband lying on top of her, remains flat over her in a manner that he covers her body with his.

- Some other permitted positions include:

  1. Standing position.
  2. Sitting position .

3. The rear-entry position – The wife lies on her front with her back facing her husband and the husband is on top of her.
4. The side-by-side position.
5. The woman to be on top of her husband whilst he is lying on his back.

■ Those prohibited occasions to have intercourse are:

1. When the woman is in the state of menstruation.
2. When the woman is in the state of post natal bleeding
3. In the state of Ihrām.
4. During I'tikāf.
5. Whilst fasting.

■ The disliked times of having intercourse are:

1. Having intercourse whilst in the need of relieving oneself.
2. Whilst the stomach is full.
3. Whilst the woman is pregnant or breastfeeding although it is permitted to do so.

■ Prohibited acts:

1. Oral sex.
2. Intercourse in the anal passage.
3. Facing the Qiblah.
4. To talk unnecessarily, but if it is to arouse one another for intercourse and in concealment so that nobody is able to hear, then it is permissible otherwise not.

5. The husband to intentionally drink his wife's milk.
6. To use food during foreplay.
7. Using sex aids that will cause harm to the couple.
8. Flogging and bondage.

■ When the husband has entered his penis inside his wife's vagina, then even if he has ejaculated he should not withdraw it until his wife has reached to her climax.

■ When the genitals of the couple meet (the helmet of the penis enters the vagina), then Ghusl will instantly become compulsory upon them both whether the man or the woman ejaculated or not.

■ After the man has ejaculated then the Du'ā to be read is:

$$ اَللّٰهُمَّ لَا تَجْعَلْ لِلشَّيْطَانِ فِيْمَا رَزَقْتَنَا نَصِيْباً $$

Translation: O Allāh! Do not grant the Shaytān a share in what (i.e. offspring) You bless us with.

Section Three: Contraception

■ There are two types of contraception:

Irreversible – The couple undergo a surgical operation in order to eliminate the possibility of childbirth permanently. This is totally prohibited in Islām and in doing so, they will become extremely sinful. However, in the case of extreme necessity where life and death is involved and also advised by an expert Muslim doctor then it would be permissible.

Reversible – To use such methods that control birth temporarily. This usually creates a barrier between the sperm meeting the egg, hence, the egg doesn't get fertilized. The Sahābahs ﷺ would practice the Azl method which means to withdraw the penis before ejaculation. Under normal circumstances it is Makrooh-e-Tanzeehi to practice all those reversible forms that only create a barrier between the sperm meeting the egg.

- If reversible contraception is practiced due to the following reasons then it will not render it Makrooh-e-Tanzeehi:

  1. The woman is so weak that she is unable to bear the pressure of further pregnancy.
  2. The wife is temporarily residing so far away that by conceiving it will cause difficulty.
  3. The couple are on the verge of separating.
  4. To space out children to give equal attention but not to follow the trend or custom.
  5. An existing child's health is very severe such that by conceiving another baby, it will cause difficulties.
  6. Due to the corrupt and prevalent immoral practices within the society, it will be difficult to safeguard the Imān of the children, hence contraception is practiced to limit the number of children.

- If such reversible methods come into effect after the fertilization of the egg, then they are not permissible (e.g. abortion).

- To practice reversible contraception for the fear of poverty is totally unlawful and extremely sinful.

- If the husband intends to practice (the permitted forms of) reversible contraception then it is necessary for him to obtain his wife's consent. If he practices contraception whilst she disapproves of it then he may become sinful for violating her right.

Section Four: Miscellaneous

- Some people assume that it is forbidden to have intimate relations on certain nights for instance, the fourteenth night or during the night of the full moon etc. All these assumptions have no basis in the Shari'ah.

- It is permissible for the husband and wife to look at each other's private parts, however it is better not to.

- To use sex aids or toys or anything to arouse the couple are permitted as long as it will not cause any harm to them nor are such aids in the form of animate objects.

Note: Using such aids is a detailed discussion hence it is advisable that each case is discussed with a knowledgeable scholar.

- If the husband is out and will return home late at night then he must inform his wife in advance when he will return home.

Chapter Eleven: Equality between Multiple Wives

■ Allāh ﷻ states in the Holy Qur'ān, "Marry those women whom you like, twos, threes or fours. But if you fear that you will not maintain justice between them then (marry only) one (woman) or the bondswomen you own. This will be closer to abstaining from injustice." (4:3)

■ It is permitted for a man to have multiple wives with an upper limit of four. This is conditional that a man is able to do justice between them.

■ To do justice between multiple wives is compulsory upon a man. In a Hadeeth there is severe warning for those men that fail to do justice between them. Sayyidunā Abū Hurairah ؓ relates that the Holy Prophet ﷺ said, "If a man has two wives and does not maintain justice between them then he will come on the Day of Judgement with one side (of his body) paralyzed." (Nasai, Abū Dāwood, Tirmizi)

■ Having multiple wives is no small matter rather it is a risk, hence careful consideration must be made before taking this step. If a person is certain that matters will aggravate further then he must abstain from it.

■ Justice should be maintained between wives whether they are both virgins or not or one is a virgin and the other one is not. If he spent one night with one then he must spend one night with the other and if two nights with one then two nights with the other. In short, however many nights he spends with one, he must spend the same amount with the other.

- However much expenditure, jewellery etc the husband gives to one wife, the other wife has the full right to demand the same.

- If the husband marries for the second time whilst in the wedlock of another, he must still do justice between them.

- The co-wife can give up her rights whenever she wishes and can reclaim them back whenever she wishes.

- Although legally it is not necessary for a man to seek permission from his first wife to marry the second time but morally he is advised to do so. In doing so morally, it will dispel further disputes between the couple.

- Equality between wives is only legally compulsory during the night and not during the day. If he remains longer with one wife than the other during the day then there will be no sin. However morally he should do justice in this also. If the husband works throughout the night then he must do justice during the day.

- Justice is not necessary in terms of sexual relations and neither is it required in terms of love and affection as this is natural. However, this should not be a leeway for the husband to abandon one wife as he is still obliged to do justice with her.

- When travelling, it is Sunnah to draw lots between the wives to see which wife will accompany him on the journey.

Chapter Twelve: Huqooquz Zawjain (the Rights of the Husband and Wife)

- Allāh ﷻ states in the Holy Qur'ān, "Men are caretakers of women since Allāh has made some of them excel others and because of the wealth they have spent (on their wives)." (4:34)

  "And for them (women) are similar rights to what they owe (rights to their husbands) and for men is a degree higher over them (in terms of responsibilities)." (2:228)

- Marriage is a gift from Allāh ﷻ whereby the married couple derive benefit from one another. There are many blessings in marriage, but it is accompanied by many responsibilities also. Allāh ﷻ and His Messenger ﷺ have outlined in great detail the rights and responsibilities of both the husband and wife.

- One of the most integral ingredients for a successful marriage is to recognise and fulfill each other's rights. It is wrong for a person to become obsessed with one's own rights whilst neglecting the others. In a Hadeeth the Holy Prophet ﷺ said, "None amongst you is a complete believer until he desires for his (Muslim) brother what he desires for himself." (Bukhāri)

The rights of the wife over her husband

- Allāh ﷻ states in the Holy Qur'ān, "And live with them with courteousness." (4:19)

The Holy Prophet ﷺ said, "O People! Fear Allāh ﷻ with regards to your wives. You have taken them into your marriage upon a pledge to Allāh ﷻ and through the command of Allāh ﷻ have they become Halāl for you."

(Bukhāri)

The Holy Prophet ﷺ also said, "The most complete believers are those who have the most excellent character, and the good amongst you are those who are good to their wives." (Tirmizi)

- The fundamental Huqooq (rights) that Islām has given to a wife over her husband are as follows:

1. Husne Khulq – To treat her with kindness, love, respect, nobility, happiness and good character.
2. To endure patience over her mistakes and overlook her natural faults and shortcomings. He admonishes her politely and does not lose his temper over her.
3. Not to be suspicious or distrustful to his wife and neither should he be negligent with regards to her.
4. To adopt moderation when spending on her, not to be stingy and neither be extravagant.
5. Islamic education – It is compulsory for the husband to teach her the obligations of Deen. This includes to teach her all the rules of the regular prayers, fasting, menstruation and post natal bleeding, Halāl and Harām issues, providing her the fundamental teachings of the Holy Qur'ān and the Sunnah of the Holy Prophet ﷺ, to avoid sins and innovations etc.

6. To fulfill her sexual needs and not to practice the permitted forms of contraception without her permission.
7. To maintain justice between multiple wives.
8. Not to physically, verbally, emotionally or sexually abuse her, not to cheat on her and neither take unfair advantage over her loyalty and faithfulness.
9. Not to divorce her unless there is an extreme necessity. This should always be used as a last resort.
10. To provide her adequate expenses and living accommodation.
11. Allow her to meet her Mahram relatives.
12. Not to reveal her private affairs to anyone else.
13. Never to humiliate her nor force her out of the house.
14. Not to instruct her to do what is beyond her capacity.
15. To defend her honour.
16. Not to complain about her unnecessarily.
17. Not to force or threaten her to do the household duties or to cook.

The Rights of the Husband over his Wife

■ The Holy Prophet ﷺ said, "Whichever woman establishes her five regular prayers, fasts in the month of Ramadhān, protects her chastity and obeys her husband will enter Paradise through whichever door she desires." (Mishkāt)

■ The Holy Prophet ﷺ said, "A woman who dies whilst her husband is pleased with her will enter Paradise." (Tirmizi)

■ The rights of the husband over the wife are as follows:

1. She must obey her husband in every lawful matter and adopt good manners towards him.
2. She must not demand anything that is beyond his capacity and means.
3. Not to leave the house without the consent of her husband.
4. Not to allow a stranger to enter the house without his permission.
5. Not to give anyone his wealth or belongings without his permission.
6. To safeguard his wealth, children and belongings during his absence.
7. Not to offer any optional prayer or fast without his permission.
8. If the husband desires to have sexual relationship with her then she must not refuse unless there are Shar'ee preventions like menstruation, post natal bleeding or is extremely ill.
9. Never to despise or ridicule her husband because of his looks or poverty.
10. To admonish her husband politely if he breaks any of the commands of Allāh ﷻ.
11. Not to call her husband by his name.
12. Not to complain about her husband to anyone unnecessarily.
13. Never to be abusive or disrespectful towards him nor cheat on him.
14. To defend his honour.
15. To treat his parents like her own parents and never to dispute with them.

Chapter Thirteen: General Advice about Marriage

- Allāh ﷻ states in the Holy Qur'ān, "And if you fear breach between them both (the husband and wife) then appoint arbitrators; one from his family and one from her family. If they both wish for peace Allāh will cause their reconciliation, Allāh is Most High, Most Great." (4:35)

- Between every married couple, disagreements and quarrels do occur. Islām has set guidelines on how to deal with them.

- If one of them violates the commands of Allāh ﷻ then the first step is to admonish them. This should be done in a polite but straight forward manner. Wisdom should be adopted when advising. They should never become extremely temperamental as this will cause further problems.

- If the matter still gets out of hand then the next step is to separate their beds.

- If this does not work then the third step is to appoint a family member to engage as an arbitrator who is non-judgmental, wise and has a good understanding of the situation, who will listen to both party's views neutrally and come up with an appropriate decision according to the Shari'ah. If appointing such an arbitrator within the family is not possible then this matter should be referred to a reliable and knowledgeable scholar.

74

- After trying the above mentioned avenues, if the couple still do not come to a mutual settlement and the situation is such that they can no longer maintain their marriage then the final resort is divorce. (This will be discussed in details in chapter fourteen Inshā-Allāh).

- It is not advisable to use hitting as a resort. It is stated in a Hadeeth that the Holy Prophet ﷺ never in his entire life raised his noble hands against any woman.

- Always ensure that the husband and wife fulfill one another's compulsory rights (as explained in chapter twelve). Fear Allāh ﷻ when carrying out responsibilities and adopt good manners towards one another.

- It is important that the couple never quarrel in the presence of their children because this will also affect their lives in the future. The couple should always confine their disagreements and quarrels between themselves for instance, in their bedroom.

- It is important to overlook the natural faults of one's spouse and observe the good qualities. This will hopefully strengthen the bond and affection between them. If there is one defect in them then Allāh ﷻ has surely created many good qualities in them.

- If a matter has already been settled between the couple then as a general factor, it must not be disclosed again. The matter should be left alone and thereafter move on.

- If the husband or wife committed a mistake and thereafter sincerely repented then as long as the mistake is not perpetrated again, it is not appropriate to continuously insult or ridicule them.

Chapter Fourteen: The System of Divorce in Islām

Section One: Issuing a Divorce

- Allāh 🕮 states in the Holy Qur'ān, "Divorce is twice, now either retain her with goodness or release her with kindness." (2:229)

- In the eyes of Allāh 🕮 divorce is one of the worst of the permissible things. It is mentioned in a Hadeeth related by Sayyidunā Abdullāh Ibn Umar 🕮 that the Holy Prophet 🕮 said, "The worst of Halāl things in the sight of Allāh 🕮 is divorce." (Abū Dāwood)

  In another Hadeeth the Holy Prophet 🕮 said, "Marry but do not divorce, verily the Arsh (throne) of Allāh 🕮 shakes with divorce." (Abū Dāwood)

- If the husband and wife can no longer maintain their marriage and the nature of the situation is such that if they live together, matters will deteriorate, then as a final resort they can go through a divorce. However, careful consideration must be made before divorcing. Whenever there is an opportunity to avoid it then it is best to avoid it.

- In Islām, the man has the authority to divorce as long as he is sane and Bāligh (mature). Islām does not recognise the divorce pronounced by the woman, hence if she divorces then it will not come into effect.

- If a person whilst in his sleep divorces his wife, it will not come into effect.

- It is not necessary for the couple to go through a court case for divorce if they don't want to. In Islām divorce is simple. When the husband pronounces a divorce to his wife she must thereafter observe her Iddah (waiting period) which is three full menstrual cycles or until she gives birth if pregnant (this will be discussed in details in chapter sixteen Inshā-Allāh). After completing her Iddah she is now eligible to marry someone else. A woman who is divorced is known as a Mutallaqah.

- Divorce will also occur if the husband wrote it on a paper or signed a divorce paper or via text message or email even if he did not pronounce it verbally with the condition that he acknowledges and confesses to it and has written it of his own freewill. If the man was compelled to write or sign a divorce paper (or even to text or email) then it will not come into effect as long as he does not pronounce it verbally.

- If a man is forced to divorce his wife verbally then it will come into effect. One scheme could be to suffix the word 'Inshā-Allāh' after the word 'divorce' instantly in the same breath, in this case the divorce will not take place.

- If a man consumed Harām substance like alcohol or drugs and thereafter, in the state of intoxication issued a divorce then it will take place. But if someone became intoxicated through consuming a Halāl substance and issues a divorce in this state, then it will not take place.

- Issuing a divorce in the state of anger will come into effect and the wife will be divorced.

- There are three types of divorces that a man issues:

1. **Talāq-e-Ahsan** - To pronounce one divorce to the wife in that pure period in which they had no intimate relationship. This method is the most recommended way of divorcing one's wife.

2. **Talāq-e-Sunnah or Hasan** - To pronounce three divorces separately whereby issuing one divorce in each of the three pure periods to one's wife with whom he has already had an intimate relationship with.

3. **Talāq-e-Bid'ah:** To either pronounce all three divorces in one sitting or in one pure period without any intervals of menstrual period or to issue a divorce whilst she is menstruating. This is one of the worst and detestable forms of divorce and in doing so the divorce will take place. However the man will also become very sinful.

- The divorce that occurs upon a woman is of three kinds:

1. **Talāq-e-Raj'ee (Revocable Divorce)** - When the husband pronounces one or two divorces to his wife who he has already had an intimate relationship with. The ruling would be that whilst the wife is observing her waiting period, if both of them decide to reconcile then they can do so without remarrying. However, if her waiting period has completed and thereafter they decide to reconcile, then they cannot do so unless they remarry because at this point their marriage has officially ended and they are now complete strangers to one another.

2. **Talāq-e-Bā'in (Irrevocable Divorce)** - To divorce by using certain terminologies that can indicate towards divorce as well as something else. Such terms are referred to as Kināyah (ambiguous). After the completion of her waiting period she is free to marry someone else. However, if they decide to reconcile then it is necessary to renew their marriage irrespective of whether they reconcile within her waiting period or after.

3. **Talāq-e-Mughalladha (Absolute Irrevocable Divorce)** - To issue three divorces either in one sitting or separately. In this case the couple can no longer rejoin with one another whether during her waiting period or after. However, if the wife married another man and had an intimate relationship with him, thereafter he either divorced her or passed away, then after completing her waiting period from her second husband she decides to marry her first husband then it would be permissible. This is known as Halālah.

Note: To intentionally practice Halālah is not permissible. It is related in a Hadeeth that the one who practices Halālah and for the one whom Halālah is practiced are both cursed (Mishkāt). Halālah would only be permissible if it was done without it being pre-planned.

■ The terms that a man uses to issue a divorce are of 2 types:

1. **Sareeh (Clear Terms)** - To use such categorical terms that only indicate towards divorce and nothing else. For instance Zaid said to his wife, 'I divorce you or I have given

you Talāq.' Then the divorce will take place regardless of his intention. The intention of a man is not taken into consideration. If a man says to his wife, 'I divorce you' then only one will occur but if he repeated the word 'divorce' three times then three will occur and similarly twice.

2. **Kināyah (Ambiguous Terms):** To use such terms that can indicate to divorce as well as something else. For instance, ' Go away from me, get out of my house, go and live with your parents, I have nothing to do with you, stay away from me, you are fārigh etc.' Such terms can be used either for divorce or something else. In this case the intention and situation are both considered. If by using such terms the husband's intention was to divorce his wife or by looking at the situation the only possible meaning could be divorce and nothing else then the wife will be divorced. The divorce that will occur on the wife in the case of Kināyah will be Talāq-e-Bā'in. But if the husband's intention was not to divorce at all then it will not take place.

■ By using clear terms, divorce will take place whether it is issued seriously or as a joke.

■ If the husband uses a past or present tense then divorce will occur i.e. 'I divorced you' or 'I divorce you.' If future tense was used then it will not occur i.e. 'I intend to divorce you, I'm going to divorce you or I will divorce you,'

■ It is a sin to issue a divorce whilst the woman is menstruating nevertheless the divorce will still occur.

- For divorce to occur it is necessary to pronounce it verbally or written. A person just intending to divorce his wife in the heart but not uttering anything is not classed as divorce.

- A man calling his wife saying 'O divorcee' then it will occur even as a joke.

Section Two: To divorce before an intimate relationship

- If the husband divorced his wife (even if once) instantly after the marriage and before an intimate relationship or Khalwat-e-Saheehah (which means to remain secluded at such a time or place that would not Islamically or medically prevent them from having intercourse) then a Talāq-e-Bā'in will occur. The wife will not observe any waiting period and is free to marry someone else. It will only be compulsory for the woman to observe a waiting period if either of the two things; intimate relationship or Khalwat-e-Saheehah occurred.

- If before intimacy or Khalwat-e-Saheehah the husband pronounced three divorces altogether in one sitting then this will become Talāq-e-Mughalladha. She will not observe any waiting period and neither can they reconcile unless after Halālah.

- If the marriage was Fāsid (invalid according to the Shari'ah) on the account of which they separated then if the separation took place before an intimate relationship the woman is not obliged to observe an Iddah. However, if an intimate relationship did take place then she must observe an Iddah. Khalwat-e-Saheehah will not count as anything because this is only considered in that marriage which is valid in Islām. This separation will result in a Talāq-e-Bā'in.

Section Three: To issue 3 Divorces altogether in one sitting

■ Allāh ﷻ states in the Holy Qur'ān,"So if he divorces her (the third time) then it will be unlawful for him (to marry her) until she marries another husband besides him." (2:230)

■ If the husband issues three divorces either separately or all at once then all three will come into effect. There are many authentic Ahādeeth that give evidence of this:

1. Sayyidah Ā'ishah ﷺ relates that a man pronounced three divorces to his wife, so she married another man (after completing her Iddah) and this man then divorced her (before an intimate relationship). She asked the Messenger of Allāh ﷺ whether it was lawful for her to return to the first husband? The Holy Prophet ﷺ said to her no until she has an intimate relationship. (Bukhāri)

2. Layth reports from Nāfi that when Sayyidunā Abdullāh Ibn Umar ﷺ was asked regarding three divorces then he would reply, "If one or two divorces (then they could have rejoined) because the Messenger of Allāh ﷺ instructed me to do this (i.e. rejoin), but if he divorced her thrice then she becomes Harām upon him until she marries someone else." (Bukhāri)

3. The above Hadeeth is further explained in another lengthy Hadeeth reported by Sayyidunā Abdullāh Ibn Umar ؓ that once he divorced his wife whilst she was menstruating and he intended to divorce her twice more. The Holy Prophet ﷺ was informed of this act and instructed him to rejoin with her (to revoke that one divorce) and thereafter divorce her in her pure period. Sayyidunā Abdullāh Ibn Umar ؓ thereafter asked, "O Messenger of Allāh ﷺ, if I divorce her thrice then can I rejoin with her?" He said, "No! The wife will now become separate from you and you will become sinful." (Dār-Qutni)

4. Sayyidunā Umar Ibn Khattāb ؓ made it a consensus during his Khilāfah when this issue reached to epidemic level and all of the Sahābahs ؓ agreed to this unanimously.

- Once the divorce reaches to three whether they are issued all at once or separately then it becomes Mughalladha. It would no longer be permissible for them to rejoin unless through means of Halālah that is not pre-planned.

- It must be remembered that when a man issues one divorce and thereafter reconciles with his wife, now he only has two divorces remaining throughout their married life. Once the remaining two divorces are issued whether at once or separately then it becomes Mughalladha. It is a similar case with Talāq-e-Bā'in i.e. once he has issued one Talāq-e-Bā'in and thereafter renewed his marriage with his wife, he only has two remaining. Once the remaining two are issued they can no longer rejoin.

Section Four: To divorce with conditions

- If the husband made the divorce conditional then the moment the condition is fulfilled, the divorce will immediately take effect. After stating the condition the husband cannot take it back. For instance, if Zaid said to his wife, "If you enter the house then you are divorced," then the moment she enters the house, divorce will take place. Even if he retracts from his statement, the divorce will still take place the moment she enters.

- If a man says to a woman, "The moment I marry you, you are divorced" then the moment he marries her Talāq-e-Bā'in will take place because she is divorced before intimate relations and Khalwat-e-Saheehah. However, if he marries her for the second time then divorce will not come into effect again.

- If Zaid said to his wife, 'If you do such and such thing then two divorces' or 'one divorce' or 'three divorces' then whatever amount he specified, upon the fulfillment of that thing that many divorces will occur.

- If a woman decided to go out of her home but the husband said, 'don't go', she refused to listen to him and then he said, 'If you go out then you are divorced' then the ruling would be that if she goes out immediately, divorce will take effect but if she emerges after a period of time then it will not come into effect. It would not mean that she can never go out but only at that instant. However, if he said, "Whenever you emerge from the house you are divorced" then however many times she goes out of the house, that many divorces will take place.

84

Chapter Fifteen: Khula

- Allāh ﷻ states in the Holy Qur'ān, "And if you fear that they would not maintain the limits of Allāh (i.e. marriage) then there is no sin upon them both in what she (the wife) gives up to secure her release." (2:229)

- If the couple cannot maintain their marriage any longer and the husband refuses to issue a divorce then it would be permissible for the wife to give some money, item etc that they agree upon or pardon her right of the dowry (that is still due on the husband) in exchange of releasing herself from his wedlock. For instance the wife says to the husband, 'I will give you this much money and you re-lease me from your wedlock with Khula' or she says, 'I will forsake my right of dowry that is outstanding and in return you release me' and the husband agrees then this would be permissible as mentioned in the verse of the Ho-ly Qur'ān above. This in Shari'ah is known as Khula.

- Once Khula has been agreed between them, it now be-comes compulsory upon the wife to give the amount to her husband that was agreed upon. The separation that occurs will be Talāq-e-Bā'in. In other words they can no longer rejoin thereafter unless they renew their marriage. She will now observe her waiting period and thereafter can marry elsewhere.

- When the couple agree to this then it is necessary for the couple to be in the same gathering, for instance if the wife says to her husband, 'I will give you this much amount of money and you give me Khula.' The husband then walked away from that gathering and came back after a while and said, 'I agree' then Khula will not take place. Similarly if she walked away and then the husband accepts, Khula will also not take place.

- Once the couple agree upon Khula then with the exception of providing expenses for the wife during her waiting period, all other marital rights of one another are automatically dropped. For instance, if the husband has not yet paid her the dowry then after Khula she will no longer become entitled to it. But if she already received it then that will belong to her. The husband cannot reclaim it after Khula.

- During her waiting period it is still necessary for the husband to provide her expenses (this will be discussed in detail in chapter seventeen Inshā-Allāh). However, if she forsakes this right then this will also be dropped.

- If the husband said to his wife, 'I do Khula with you,' and the wife agreed in the same gathering (likewise visa-versa) but no specific amount of money was agreed then if the husband has not yet paid her the dowry then that will be dropped, but if he has already paid her then all other marital rights will be dropped except the financial expenses during her waiting period.

- If Khula was done on the account of the husband's guilt then it will be an act of great sin for him to accept the money in exchange and he will also become sinful of remitting the dowry for Khula which was due upon him. It will not be permissible for him to use that money for himself because he was in the wrong.

- If the woman was in the wrong then it is preferable for the husband not to agree upon an amount of money which exceeds that of the dowry. It would be better for him to forsake the dowry for Khula if it is still due. If he still accepted the excess amount then it would be permissible.

- If the husband forced or threatened his wife to do Khula then it will be regarded as divorce and not Khula. It will not be necessary for the wife to give money to her husband and neither will the dowry be dropped. The dowry will still remain a debt upon the husband if it is still outstanding.

- All of the abovementioned cases will only apply if the term Khula was used or the wife said, 'I will pay you this much and in return you release me.' If the word divorce was used rather than Khula then the rules of Khula will not apply i.e. all marital rights of one another will not be dropped like dowry etc. If money was agreed in exchange of divorcing her then the divorce that will. occur will be Talāq-e-Bā'in.

Chapter Sixteen: Iddah (Waiting Period)

Section One: The Iddah of a Divorced Woman

- Allāh ﷻ states, "And divorced women will keep them-selves waiting for three menstruations." (2:228)

  "O you who believe! When you marry believing women and then you divorced them before you touch them (intimate relationship), then there is no period for you to count on them, so give them a gift and release them in a handsome manner." (33:49)

  "O Prophet! When you (people) divorce women then di-vorce them at a time of their period of Iddah (may start), and count their Iddah and fear Allāh your Lord, do not drive them out of their homes and neither should they (i.e. the women) emerge (themselves)." (65:1)

  "And those women amongst you that have despaired of (further) menstruation, if you are in doubt then their Id-dah is three months as well as those who have not yet menstruated. And as for those pregnant ones, their term (Iddah) is until they give birth to their child. And whoever fears Allāh, He brings about ease for him in his affair."(65:4)

- If a woman is either divorced, agrees to Khula, the mar-riage is dissolved (faskh) or the husband passed away then in all these instances the woman must observe a wait-ing period which is known as Iddah in Shari'ah. The rul-ing is that whilst she is observing her Iddah or waiting period, she is not permitted to observe it anywhere else besides her husband's residence. During her Iddah if the husband is alive then it is compulsory upon him to provide her with the necessary expenses which include food, clothing, expenditure and accommodation.

- It is only compulsory for a divorcee to observe her Iddah if after the marriage the couple had an intimate relationship or Khalwat-e-Saheehah. If any of the above two cases did not take place at all after the marriage then she is not obliged to observe any Iddah when divorced and is free to marry elsewhere.

- During her Iddah, it is not permissible for her to marry someone else and neither to propose to someone until her Iddah has completed.

- There are four types of Iddah that a woman observes:
  1. Three menstruations.
  2. Three months.
  3. Pregnancy until she gives birth.
  4. Four months and ten days.

- A woman who menstruates has either been divorced, agreed upon Khula or marriage is dissolved, then her waiting period will be three full menstrual cycles. If a woman does not menstruate then her waiting period will be three months.

- If a woman is pregnant then her waiting period will be until she gives birth. This is applicable to a divorcee and a woman whose husband has passed away.

- If, Allāh ﷻ forbid, a pregnant woman has a miscarriage then there are one of two situations:

1. If she had a miscarriage upon four months or more then her waiting period has completed and the blood that discharges thereafter will be Nifās (post-natal bleeding).

2. If miscarriage occurred prior to four months then her waiting period will not be completed. In this case the blood that discharges will not be classed as Nifās and her waiting period will now switch to three menstruations. If the bleeding occurred for three consecutive days and night then it will be classed as menstruation otherwise not. When she begins her first menstruation, her new Iddah will recommence.

- If a woman was observing her Iddah of three months but during this period, she begins to menstruate then her Iddah will now change to three menstruations. She will now resume her Iddah to menstruation and the previous days or months observed will become void.

- If a man divorced his wife whilst she was menstruating then that menstruation will not be included. Rather her Iddah will begin from the following menstruation.

Section two: The Iddah of a woman whose husband has passed away

- Allāh ﷻ states in the Holy Qur'ān, "Those amongst you pass away and leave behind wives (as widows), they (the wives) will keep themselves waiting for four months and ten days."(2:234)

- If a woman has become a widow and she is not pregnant then her waiting period will be four months and ten days. However, if she is pregnant then her waiting period will complete when she gives birth.

- She must observe her Iddah in her husband's home and should not emerge from there unless due to extreme necessity.

- Whilst observing her Iddah at home she is free to move around anywhere at home. It is not necessary for her to be restricted to her bedroom etc.

- If the wife was divorced and was observing her three menstrual cycles but during this period, for instance after completing one menstruation, her husband passed away, now she will observe the longest of the two periods i.e. if four months and ten days is longer than the remaining two menstruations, she must now observe the Iddah of four months and ten days.

- It is not compulsory to provide expenses to the widow; she will spend upon herself from what she receives from inheritance or from any other source of income that she receives. However, if someone wishes to take the responsibility to provide for her then it is immensely rewarding.

- Once her Iddah has completed then she is free to marry someone else. It is wrong to believe that a widow can never marry in the future.

Section Three: What to do during Iddah

- A woman who has been given either a Talāq-e-Bā'in, Mughalladha, the marriage has been dissolved or a woman whose husband has passed away then during her Iddah, she cannot emerge from her home unless due to extreme necessity nor marry another person and neither adorn herself.

- Not to adorn herself includes; to abstain from applying fragrance, surma, oil, mehndi, wearing attractive clothes, jewellery, silk. However, she is permitted to have a bath.

- A woman who has been given a Talāq-e-Raj'ee can adorn herself as she is permitted to rejoin with her husband during her Iddah without renewing the marriage. However, during the Iddah she is not permitted to emerge from her home unless due to extreme necessity and nor marry someone else.

- It will only become compulsory upon a woman not to adorn herself if the contract of marriage was done according to the Shari'ah. If the marriage was invalid according to Shari'ah (Nikāh Fāsid) e.g. contracted without any witnesses, and thereafter the husband either passed away or the marriage was dissolved then during her Iddah she is permitted to adorn herself.

- In the case of Nikāh Fāsid, if the man passed away after an intimate relationship then she will merely observe three menstrual periods.

Chapter Seventeen: Expenses and Custody of the Child

■ Allāh ﷻ states in the Holy Qur'ān, "It is the obligation of the one to whom the child belongs to (the father) that he provides food and clothing for them with fairness." (2:233)

"Men are caretakers of women since Allāh has made some of them excel over the others and because of the wealth they have spent (on their women)." (4:34)

■ In Islām it is the sole responsibility upon the man to provide expenses; food, clothing, shelter for his wife, children and parents. If other Mahram relatives are in extreme need and there is nobody to cater for them besides him then he must provide for them also. If he neglects this responsibility then he will become extremely sinful.

Section One: Expenses to one's Wife

■ It is obligatory upon the man to provide the necessary expenses for his wife even though she is rich or an Ahl-e-Kitāb. The general principle to remember is that the moment the wife moves to her husband's home it becomes the duty upon the husband to provide for her with the basic and necessary provisions.

■ After the marriage, if the woman refuses to move to her husband's home for a genuine reason e.g. the husband refuses to give her the dowry, even then the husband must still provide expenses for her.

- If she refuses to move to her husband's home without a Shar'ee reason or after moving she continuously emerges from her home unnecessarily, without any valid reason, or she is a Nāshizah (openly disobedient) then in all these circumstances it would not become necessary upon the husband to provide expenses for her.

Note: A valid Shar'ee reason for not moving to her husband's home includes that the husband will violate her basic rights.

- If the wife is severely ill then the husband should provide for her medication.

- When spending upon the family then moderation should always be adopted. If they are both rich then moderation according to their level and similarly if they are poor then moderation according to their standard.

- Whatever expenses the husband provides, he cannot re-claim them back. If the husband is very stingy and refuses to spend on his wife then it is permissible for her to take some money without his consent, but only that amount that will suffice her.

- It is not legally compulsory in Islām for the wife to do the household duties or cook food. However, morally in doing so there is great reward because women are the best in this area. When the Holy Prophet 🌸 arranged his daughter, Sayyidah Fātimah's 🌸 marriage with Sayyidunā Ali 🌸then the Holy Prophet 🌸 distributed their responsibilities for them. He instructed Sayyidunā Ali ☘ to be responsible for the outdoor affairs (i.e. to earn adequate income for the home) while Sayyidah Fātimah ☘ for the domestic affairs. We all should learn from this example.

- If for some genuine reason the wife refuses to do the household duties, for instance, she is severely ill then the husband or any other person cannot compel her.

- It is not legally compulsory for the daughter in-law to serve her in-law parents or other family members like her brother in-laws and sister in-laws. However, in doing so there is great reward in it. If she is unable to do so then she cannot be forced nor threatened.

Section Two: The wife visiting her parents

- If a woman after obtaining the consent from her husband goes to visit her parents then throughout her duration of visit it is necessary upon the husband to provide for her necessary expenses.

- It is permitted for the wife to visit her parents or her parents to come over to visit her at least once in a week. The husband cannot put any restrictions and must also provide for her necessary expenses. Besides this, if the visitation is very frequent (more than once a week) such that it will cause difficulty or inconvenience to the husband or to their marriage life then he can put restrictions but using appropriate measures.

- The husband cannot put any restriction if any other Mahram relatives come to visit or she goes to visit them once in a year and the husband must provide her the expenses. If the visitation beyond once a year causes any inconvenience to him or affect their marriage life then he can put restrictions but using appropriate measures.

- If the wife wishes to speak to her parents or to her Mahram relatives over the phone or communicate via e-mail etc. then generally the husband should not prevent her (unless it will cause any inconvenience to the marriage).

- If the wife's parents or either of them are severely ill and there is nobody to cater for them, then if the wife wants to go to serve her parents even if it means to go more than once in a week, then the husband should not prevent her. He should provide her with financial support even if they are non-Muslims. If her husband prevents her she is still permitted to go but in this case the husband will not be legally obliged to financially support her although it would be better for him to do so.

Section Three: Providing Accommodation

- If the wife does not want to live with any other family members in the same house, and demands a separate accommodation from all Mahram relatives so that she, her husband and children can live conveniently, then it becomes the legal responsibility upon the husband to arrange a separate accommodation that fulfils their basic requirements of living.

- If she wishes to live with other Mahram family members in the same house then she can demand a separate room for her belongings.

- If a woman is observing her Iddah of divorce etc, then she must observe it in her husband's home and the husband must provide for her expenses and accommodation. However, if she emerges herself out of the home then it will no longer be necessary upon him to provide for her.

Section Four: Expenses for children and parents

- It is compulsory upon the man to provide expenses for his children and parents even if they are non-Muslims.

- The duty upon the father to provide for his daughter remains until she gets married. However, if the daughter is either rich or is receiving sufficient income through other means then it is not compulsory for him to provide expenses for her.

- It is compulsory upon the father to provide for his son until attaining Buloogh (maturity). Once the boy has attained Buloogh and is physically and mentally capable of providing for himself, then it is no longer compulsory upon the father to provide for him. However, if after attaining Buloogh the child is physically or mentally ill or circumstances are such that he cannot provide for himself then the father must provide expenses for him.

- If the parents are poor or do not have any other source of income that is sufficient for them then the man must also provide for them. However, if they are rich or receive sufficient income through other means, then despite the fact that it is not necessary to spend on them, in doing so there is great reward.

- Regarding all other Mahram relatives if they are extremely poor and they have no other source of income then it is compulsory to provide for them otherwise not.

Section Five: Custody of the child after divorce

- If for some reason the parents separate and they have children, then the mother will have the first right of custody over the child until the boy reaches the age of seven. In the case of a girl until she is nine or menstruates. Thereafter the father can reclaim the right of custody over them.

- It is permissible for the mother to give up her right of custody to the father and likewise the father to the mother. The expenses of the child will be due upon the father even if the child is under the care of the mother.

- The mother will have the first right of the young child and if she is not alive then the maternal grandmother, if not then the paternal grandmother. If they all don't exist then real sisters, if not then maternal step-sisters, thereafter the paternal step-sister, if they do not exist then the maternal aunt and if not then the paternal aunt.

- If any of the above relatives do not exist then the father will take over the custody of the child.

- When the father has the right of custody over the child but he either passed away or himself relinquishes the responsibility for the child then after mutual compromise if the mother takes the child back then that is permissible.

- The right of custody is dropped due to one of the following reasons:

1. The mother during the custody got married to a man who is a Ghair Mahram to the child.

2. She seeks payment for taking care of the child.

3. She frequently emerges from her home such that a lack of attention is being given to the child.

4. Either of them is involved in Fisq and Fujoor (open sins and transgression) and are totally corrupt.

5. The child remains under the care of a disbeliever to the extent that he/she will be affected.

6. The custodian becomes a Murtad (an apostate).

Chapter Eighteen: Upbringing of Children in Islām

- Children are a great blessing and an honourable trust from Allāh ﷻ. Parents are responsible for upbringing them in the correct manner by following the Islamic guidelines. If the parents neglect this obligation then they will be held accountable on the Day of Judgement. The parents will receive a share of reward of the good things that a child does, similarly the parents will receive a share of the sin that the child commits.

- It is our firm belief that every child is born Māsoom (pure from sins) and upon the Deen of Fitrah i.e. Islām.

Section One: What to do when a child is born

- When a child is born then it is Sunnah to give the Adhān in the right ear and Iqāmah in the left. The purpose of this is so that the first words that reach into the child's ears are the words of Allāh ﷻ. This is what the Holy Prophet ﷺ did when his grandson, Sayyidunā Hasan Ibn Ali ؓ was born.

- Performing Tahneek –a pious person should chew a date and draw some of it on to his finger, then put it gently into the newborn's mouth, moving the finger slightly to the right and left. It is also Sunnah to pray for the well-being of that child.

- On the seventh day of the birth, the child's head should be shaved and the hair weighed. That weight of silver value should be then given to charity.

- Aqeeqah should be performed on the seventh day which is to sacrifice one goat or sheep for a girl and two for a boy. If one cannot afford to sacrifice two for a boy then one will suffice. If a person contributes towards a large animal then one share for a girl and two shares for a boy. The meat can be distributed either raw or cooked for the family members, relatives, neighbours and friends.

- It is amongst the important rights of a child that he/she is given a good name. The Holy Prophet ﷺ said, "The rights that a child has over the father is to teach him (or her) good manners and give him a good name." (Baihaqi)

- It is preferable to name the child with the same name as the Prophets ﷺ. The Holy Prophet ﷺ said, "Give yourselves the names of the Prophets." (Abū Dāwood)

- Girls should be given the names of the pious women of the past or the names of the Sahābiyāt.

- It is Sunnah to name the child on the seventh day.

- It is Sunnah to do Khatna (circumcision) for a boy which means to remove the foreskin from the tip of his penis.

Section Two: Rewards of giving birth to daughters and bringing them up.

- It is very unfortunate that some people feel disgraced and upset upon the birth of a daughter. In Islām having a daughter is a great blessing. Sayyidunā Abdullāh Ibn

101

Abbās ❀ narrates that the Holy Prophet ❀ said, "Whosoever is blessed with a girl and did not inflict (any form of) harm upon her, nor did he disgrace her and neither did he give preference to sons over her (but treated them equally), then Allāh ❀ will enter him into Paradise with her." (Ahmad)

■ Sayyidāh Ā'ishah ❀ relates that the Holy Prophet ❀ said, "Whoever is tested with the (responsibilities) of daughters (and fulfilled his responsibility) and treated them with kindness, then they (the daughters) will serve as a protection for him from the fire of Hell." (Bukhāri & Muslim)

■ Great rewards have been promised specifically for raising daughters. The Holy Prophet ❀ said, "If anyone raises three daughters or three sisters, teaches them manners and shows compassion towards them until Allāh ❀ makes them independent, then he will be rewarded with Paradise." Someone asked, "What is the reward of raising two?" He said, "The same is for raising two." The narrator states that if the Sahābah ❀ had asked about one daughter or sister then the Holy Prophet ❀ would have surely said the same about one also." (Tirmizi & Abū Dāwood)

Section Three: Responsibilities

1) **Monetary responsibility** – It is obligatory upon the father to spend on his own children until they are old enough to support themselves. Not only is it compulsory but also rewarding. Sayyidunā Thawbān ❀ relates that the Holy

Prophet ﷺ said, "The money that is spent in the best way is that which is spent on one's family, on one's horse in the path of Allāh ﷻ or one's companion in the path of Allāh ﷻ." (Muslim)

2) **Treating them equally** – It is compulsory for the parents to treat their children fairly. This means to avoid giving preference to one child in terms of kind treatment or giving everything to one whilst neglecting the others. As far as love is concerned then this is involuntary as this is from Allāh ﷻ. Having affection for one more than the other is not against equal treatment as long as this is not expressed through one's treatment. Sayyidunā Nu'mān Ibn Basheer ؓ relates that his father (Basheer ؓ) gave him something. His mother Umrah Bint Rawāha ؓ suggested that he appoints the Holy Prophet ﷺ as a witness in this transaction. The Holy Prophet ﷺ said, "Did you give such a gift to all your children?" He said, "No." The Holy Prophet ﷺ said, "Fear Allāh ﷻ with regards to your children and do justice between them." So he (Basheer ؓ) returned and took back what he gave (to Nu'mān ؓ).

3) **Never to curse them** – Sayyidunā Jābir ؓ relates that the Holy Prophet ﷺ said, "Do not make adverse supplications against yourselves, your children or your property lest you strike a moment when Allāh ﷻ grants what you asked for." (Muslim)

4) **Compassion and Kind Treatment** – Being compassionate towards children was a noble Sunnah of the Holy Prophet

🌸. Sayyidunā Abū Hurairah 🌸 relates that the Holy Prophet 🌸 kissed Hasan Ibn Ali 🌸 (his grandson), Aqra Ibn Hābis 🌸 remarked (upon seeing this), "I have ten children but I have never shown love to any of them." The Holy Prophet 🌸 looked at him and said, "Those that have no mercy for others then mercy will not be shown to them." (Bukhāri, Muslim)

5) **Teach them good manners and etiquettes** – Sayyidunā Saeed Ibn Ās 🌸 relates that the Holy Prophet 🌸 said, "There is no better gift that a father can give to his child than good manners." (Tirmizi)

Sayyidunā Anas 🌸 relates that the Holy Prophet 🌸 said, "Honour your children and teach them good manners."

(Ibn Mājah)

It is very important to teach our children the Sunnah conduct and manners of everything which include how to eat, drink, sleep, respecting elders, how to converse with others, dressing, performing Ibādah, never to enter without seeking permission and all other domestic and social etiquettes. When teaching children the Ādāb and manners then it was the Sunnah of the Holy Prophet 🌸 to teach them with kindness. Sayyidunā Amr Ibn Abū Salamah 🌸 narrates that when he was a child under the care of the Holy Prophet 🌸, while eating his hand would go everywhere on the plate. The Holy Prophet 🌸 said to him, "Say Bismillāh and eat with your right hand and eat what is close to you." (Bukhāri, Muslim).

Sayyidunā Anas Ibn Mālik ﷺ relates that I served the Holy Prophet ﷺ for ten years and he never said 'Uff' to me and neither did he ask me about anything that I had done, "Why did you do it?" and if I did not do anything, he never said to me, "Why didn't you do it?" (Bukhāri & Muslim). The most appropriate time to teach children manners is at the age of seven. The Holy Prophet ﷺ said teach children how to pray Salāh at the age of seven.

6) **Islamic Education** – To provide them all the necessary Islamic education to fulfil all of their obligations. It would be better and more rewarding if they study to become scholars. It is permissible to provide them secular education as long as it is not detrimental to their Deen.

7) **Spiritual Training** – To instil in them the love of Allāh ﷻ and His Messenger ﷺ, to abstain from sins and to control their carnal desires.

8) **Setting a good example for your children** – Parents are the first teachers of their children, whatever they observe in their parents they are most likely to adopt.

9) **Monitoring your children** – It is essential to monitor your children's behaviour and observe their conduct towards others. Likewise, to monitor their associates and their habits. Sayyidunā Abū Hurairah ﷺ relates that the Holy Prophet ﷺ said, "A man adopts the ways of his friends so observe (carefully) who you make friends with."

(Abū Dāwood, Tirmizi)

10) **To arrange their marriage when the time is right** – Once they have reached the age of puberty and are able to marry, then they should be married. If they are able to marry but the parents fail to do so, then if the child commits the sin of fornication, the burden of sin will be on the parent's shoulders.

Bibliography

1. **The Holy Qur'ān**
2. **Saheeh Al-Bukhāri** - by Imām Muhammad Ibn Ismā'eel Al-Bukhāri 🏵
3. **Saheeh Muslim** - by Imām Muslim 🏵
4. **Jāmi Tirmizi** - by Imām Tirmizi 🏵
5. **Sunan Abū Dāwood** - by Imām Abū Dāwood 🏵
6. **Mishkāt-ul-Masābeeh** - Allāmah Baghawi 🏵
7. **Riyād-Us-Sāliheen** - by Imām Abū Zakariyyah Yahyā Ibn Sharaf An-Nawawi 🏵
8. **Ma'ārif-ul-Hadeeth** - by Shaykh Manzoor Numāni 🏵
9. **Mazāhir Haq** - by Allāmah Muhammad Qutubudeen Khān 🏵
10. **Durrul-Mukhtār** - by Allāmah Muhammad Ibn Ali Al-Haskafi Al-Hanafi 🏵
11. **Raddul-Muhtār** - by Allāmah Ibn Ābideen As-Shāmi 🏵
12. **Fatāwa Hindiyyah**
13. **Ashraf's Blessing of Marriage**
14. **Beheshti Zewar** - by Shaykh Ashraf Ali Thānwi 🏵
15. **Kitāb-un-Nikāh** - by Shaykh Zahīr
16. **Islamic Marriage** - Shaykh Ashraf Ali Thānwi 🏵
17. **Kitābul Fatāwa** - by Shaykh Khālid Saifullāh Rahmāni
18. **Fatāwa Mahmoodiyah** - by Shaykh Mufti Mahmoodul Hasan Gangohi 🏵
19. **Islamic Guide to sexual relationship** - by Shaykh Mufti Muhammad Ibn Ādam Al-Kawthari
20. **Sexual relationship** - by Shaykh Mūsa Karmādi
21. **The Complete System of Divorce in Islām** - by Shaykh Mufti Abdul Jaleel Qāsmi
22. **The Prophet's Saying on Rearing Children** - by Shaykh Mufti Sa'eed Ahmad Pālanpūri
23. **Mukhtasar Al-Qudoori** - Imām Abul Hasan Al-Qudoori 🏵
24. **Lecture on Marriage in Islām** - by Shaykh Ibrāhīm Madani
25. **Lectures Series on Fiqh of Marriage** - by Shaykh Mufti Muhammad Ibn Ādam Al-Kawthari